MW00902473

Pro
Foundations

2

speak t00 day

1

speediom™
USA, Mexico

Sixth Edition 2019

**Published in the United States for speediom™
San Diego California**

Contact us at:
professional@speediom.com

MISSION

Speed all our students' communication **well beyond** any other system.

CORPORATE VISION

Speed up to become the ***fastest-growing language school chain***
in the northwest region of Mexico.

BOOK BREAKDOWN

CHAPTER	STRUCTURE	PAGE
	COLLEGE FRIENDS	
1	BE, POSSESSIVE ADJECTIVES	4
	THE HUNK	
2	BE, PREPOSITIONS, EITHER	13
	MY HIGH SCHOOL BUDDIES	
3	FROM, BE, ADJECTIVES	21
	WHAT ARE YOU WEARING?	
4	TO BE + WEARING, POSSESSIVE ADJ. & NAMES	27
	WHAT ARE YOU DOING?	
5	PRESENT PROGRESSIVE	36
	LOVER BOY	
6	PREPOSITIONS II / DO, DOES	42
	GUESS ???	
7	IS THERE/ARE THERE / DOES + HAVE	48
	WHAT DO I DO?	
8	DOES AND DO / JOBS	57
NOTES	NOTES/VERBS	131/163

speak t00 day

¡¡¡BUENAS NOTICIAS!!!

Hay muchas cosas que hacen que el inglés sea muchísimo más fácil de aprender que muchos otros idiomas, incluyendo el español.

Aquí te vamos a dar varios ejemplos de qué estamos hablando:

1. Tamaño: Pon atención a cuál lado es más grande, el izquierdo que está en español ó el derecho que está en inglés. Así es. En español tendemos a decir muchas palabras y 2, tendemos a hablar mucho. El inglés es más práctico y la cultura no es de hablar tanto, sino de decir más con menos.

2. Para decir "el, la, los, las" en inglés sólo se usa UNA palabra: "The"

3. Para decir: "Un, una": sólo se usa una palabra: "a"

4. Para decir adjetivos como: "Rojo, roja, rojas, rojos sólo se usa también una palabra: "Red".

5. Para preguntar en presente, pasado, futuro condicional, y subjuntivos, sólo UNA. Ejemplo:
   a) Do you EAT?
   b) Did you EAT?
   c) Will you EAT?
   d) Would you EAT?
   e) When I EAT, I´ll EAT 2.

En español se dice: Comes, comiste, Vas a comer o comerás, comerías y cuando coma, voy a comer. Y esto es sin contar que solo usamos TÚ. Si usamos yo, él, ellos, nosotros es diferente para cada persona en cada uno de esos tiempos, lo cual significa aprender 35 conjugaciones diferentes. Mientras que en inglés sólo necesitas UNA: EAT

Así que numéricamente ya tenemos varios ejemplos que harán que aprendas inglés más rápido y con mayor facilidad que otras personas aprenden otros lenguajes.

GOOD NEWS!!!!

There are many things that make English much easier to learn than many other languages, including Spanish.

Here, we´ll give you several examples of what we´re talking about.

1. Size: pay attention to which side´s bigger, the left one in Spanish or the right one in English. That´s right. In Spanish we tend to say many words and 2, we tend to speak much. English is more practical and the culture is not one of speaking so much, but saying more with less.

READY FOR ACTION?????????

THE (el, la, los, las)

The is used for singular and plural, male or female AND the thing, is SPECIFIC. Example:

The dog	The cat	The doctor	The queen
The dogs	The cats	The doctors	The queens

IN ENGLISH, "THE" IS NOT USED FOR

- A) Colors
- B) Sports
- C) Days of the week
- D) Streets, avenues, blvds

- E) Body parts
- F) Titles
- G) Spaceships, aircraft etc
- H) Abstract things
- I) Dates
- J) Seasons
- K) When generalizing
- L) Mr., Ms., Mrs
- M) Sciences or subjects (Mathematics, Economics)

A, AN (un, una)

Used for SINGULAR, male or female & when the thing, is NOT SPECIFIC. Example:

- A) Pareces chango (singular). You look like A monkey.
- B) Quiero un taco. I want A taco.
- C) Quiero una cerveza. I want A beer.
- D) Quiero tacos. I want tacos. (aquí NO usamos "A" porque es plural)

RED, FAT, BEAUTIFUL

Adjectives IN ENGLISH are singular, plural male and female.

Hermosa

- A) The lipstick is RED.
- A) The dog is FAT.
- A) The house is BEAUTIFUL.
- B) B) The lipsticks are RED.
- B) The dogs are FAT.
- B) The houses are BEAUTIFUL.

Hermosas

VERBS

We use only ONE (1) verb for all the persons in all the different tenses:

TÚ/YO	ÉL/ELLA/ELLO	ELLOS	NOSOTROS
A) Do you/I WORK?	A) Does he WORK?	A) Do they WORK?	A) Do we WORK?
B) Did you/I WORK?	B) Did he WORK?	B) Did they WORK?	B) Did we WORK?
C) Will you/I WORK?	C) Will he WORK?	C) Will they WORK?	C) Will we WORK?
D) Would you/I WORK?	D) Would he WORK?	D) Would they WORK?	D) Would we WORK?
E) When you/I WORK, you/I'll WORK well.	E) When he WORKS, he'll WORK well.	E) When they WORK, they'll WORK well.	E) When we work we'll WORK well.

AM I...
ARE YOU...
IS HE...
IS SHE...

I. WRITE.
Then repeat.

II. LET'S TRANSFORM

_____   _____
_____   _____
_____   _____
_____   *GOOD JOB !!!*

III. COMPLETE THE QUESTIONS:

Am I ___ mechanic?   Am I _____ ?
Am I ___ English student?   Am I _____ ?
Am I a _____ ?   Am I _____ ?
Am I an _____ ?

IV. REPEAT, THEN TRANSFORM.

OPTION 1	OPTION 2
	Can you tell me
	Do you know
	Please let me know
	Tell us
	Show us
	Ask him
	Ask her
	I wonder
	Do you have any idea

V. WHAT DO YOU SEE?
Write what the teacher just showed you.

_____   _____
_____   _____
_____   _____
_____   _____

VI. QUESTIONS
Write the 2 questions your teacher just showed you.

_____?
_____?

Write 4 more questions using "Where's....?" Then practice with a partner.

_____?
_____?
_____?
_____?

VII. POWERHOUSE
Write an email to a friend. Use the questions from Part IV & this, that, these, those.

To: _____

Subject: _____

_____
_____
_____
_____

VIII. WHAT DO YOU CALL......?
Answer the following questions. Then, practice with a partner. One closes his/her book.

1. What do you call *the person who **lives**   next to your house?*   NEIGHBOR   .
2. What do you call *the person who **works**   in a hospital?* _____
3. What do you call *the person who **teaches** you English?* _____
4. What do you call *the person who **drives**   a police car?* _____
5. What do you call *the person who **puts out** fires?* _____
6. What do you call *the person who **repairs**   cars?* _____

IX. WHICH ONE.....?

_____   _____
_____   _____
_____   _____
_____   _____

X. SPEED

XI. GAME

XII. DESCRIBE YOURSELF
Finally, each student describes him or herself using "I am _____" and "I am not _____"

to say why they should get a raise/promotion.

XIII. HOMEWORK
Write 10 sentences describing yourself using different adjectives

(5 affirmative and 5 negative)

I. WRITE.
Then repeat.

II. LET'S TRANSFORM

_____ _____
_____ _____
_____ _____
_____ *GOOD JOB !!!*

III. COMPLETE THE QUESTIONS:

Am I ____ mechanic?   Are you an _____?
Are you ___ nurse?   Are you_____?
Are you ___ student?   Are you _____?
Are you a _____? Are you _____?

IV. GAME

V. HOMEWORK

_____ _____
_____ _____
_____ _____
_____ _____

VI. IE	+/-	So/Neither
John's party is great.	but	and
Avatar is awesome.	but	and
This year is excellent.		
Alex and Tom are at the party.		

I am in the hospital.		
The girls are dancing.		
The kids are sick		
The chicken isn't good	but	and
The tamales aren't hot.	but	and
Alex and Tom aren't friends.	but	and
You aren't in Zurich.		
This year so hot.		
Michael Jackson and Elvis Presley aren't actors.		
We aren't tired.		

VII. PERSONALITY CHARACTERISTICS

A. Funny   ( ) A serious person who works with high standards of ethics.
B. Honest   ( ) With much power and force.
C. Dynamic   ( ) Someone or something that makes you happy.
D. Responsible   ( ) Able to be trusted to do important things or jobs.
E. Intelligent   ( ) Not flexible, not easy to be changed.
F. Professional   ( ) A person that makes people obey rules and commands.
G. Talented   ( ) A person who always says the truth, or never robs.
H. Strict   ( ) A person who always tells orders.
I. Inflexible   ( ) Smart, showing a lot of intelligence.
J. Explosive   ( ) Always active, having a lot of energy.
K. Strong   ( ) Having a talent, a special ability to do something well.
L. Commanding   ( ) Person who has a very aggressive temper.

VIII. CONVERSATION 1   audio

Mike: Linda good morning.
Linda: Hey Mike, what´s up?
Mike: Not much, just having a good time!!
Linda: Mike, I´m curious. Are you from California?
Mike: Well…yes, I am. Why?
Linda: Because you are very similar to people from the east coast.
Mike: I am?
Linda: Yes, you are.
Mike: So???
Linda: Mmm…nothing…It´s just….funny, different.
Mike: And what about you?
Linda: What about me?
Mike: Are you really from Boston?
Linda: Of course I am !! Why do you ask?
Mike: Because you are so typical of people from California.
Linda: I am?

Mike: Oh my God Linda. You definitely are.

Linda: Name 3 reasons why I am please.

Mike: OK. Number 1, you are very dynamic. Number 2, you are so tanned.....

Linda: Haaaa !!!

Mike: And number 3, you speak sooooo Californian.

Linda: Ughh. But I am a Bostonian, remember that.

Mike: Yes, with a Californian accent. Haaa.

Linda: Mike, can I ask you a few questions and get a completely honest answer?

Mike: Of course !!

Linda: Please be very direct.

Mike: No problem, you are sooo, mysterious.

Linda: OK, here we go. First question.

Mike: Wait, wait... Linda. Why are you asking me these questions?

Linda: Mike, just answer will ya? Are you honest?

Mike: I am.

Linda: Second question: Are you dynamic and responsible?

Mike: Of course I am.

Linda: Are you intelligent, professional and talented?

Mike: Linda !!!

Linda: **Are** you...Mike?

Mike: I am totally professional and talented. And...I am intelligent too. Why?

Linda: Good Mike. Please finish your school project today. Professor Collins is very strict.

Mike: Linda, I know he is very strict.

Linda: You do?

Mike: I've heard rumors that he is a little...monster.

Linda: Really??? That's funny. I don't think so.

Mike: And not only that, he is strict, inflexible, and explosive.

Linda: Explosive !!!! (angrily)

Mike: Linda, come on !!! Is his classroom afraid of him?

Linda: Mmmmm, a little.

Mike: Is his voice strong and commanding?

Linda: Of course his voice is strong and commanding; he is a teacher.

Mike: Is his face sometimes too serious?

Linda: Oh Mike, his face is serious because **he is** a serious man.

Mike: Why are you defending Professor Collins?

Linda: Because your friend Linda is Linda Collins.

Mike: Linda Collins?? You mean Professor Collins is.....

Linda: Yes, Mike. Professor Collins is my father.

Mike: Your father !!

Linda: Yes, Michael Stevens. Professor Collins **is** my father.

Mike: Well, I really appreciate your father, he is a very professional man.

Linda: Michael, say goodbye to Linda Collins.

XII. P2 (Part 1)

1

Are you from a small town?

Are you from Mexico?

Are you Mexican?

Are you and your family from Mexico?

Am I early?

Am I your teacher?

2

Are you from an English-speaking country?

What country are you from?

Are you from the U.S.?

Where are you from?

Are you from Tokyo?

What city are you from?

Are you from Europe?
Where are you from?
Are you and your family from the U.K.?
What country are you from?
Are you and your family from a Portuguese-speaking country?
Where are you from?
Are you a Canadian Citizen?
What nationality are you?

3

Are you from a southern or northern city?
Are you and your family from Mexico?
Are you parents in the U.S. or Mexico?
Are you a teacher or student?
Are you from an English-speaking country or a Spanish-speaking country?
Am I early or late?

Am I your English teacher or your Mandarin teacher?

4

Are you a student?
Are your parents in Mexico?
Are your relatives in the U.S.?
Are you from Mexico?
Are your children at school?
Are you learning English or Italian?
Are you a doctor?
Are you happy or sad today?
Are you from a big city or a small town?
Am I your neighbor?
Am I your teacher?
Am I late?
Are you studying and working?
Are you at home?

P2 (Part 2)

1

Is your name Ricardo?
Is your name _____?
Is your mother happy?
Is your best friend nice?
Is your mom beautiful?
Is your house clean?
Is your father responsible?

2

Is your name Daniel?
What´s your name?

Is your mother sad?
How is your mother?
Is your house a complete disaster?
How is your house?
Is your brother irresponsible?
Who is irresponsible?
Is your father 20 years old?
How old is he?
Is your best friend unfriendly?
What´s he like?

XIII. P3

G   *TIC TAC TOE* **(Make questions using vocabulary from exercise VI, page 2)**

I. WRITE.
Then repeat.

II. LET'S TRANSFORM

_____   _____
_____   _____
_____   _____
_____   *GOOD JOB !!!*

MOVIE

_____
_____
_____
_____
_____
_____

SPEEDY VIDEO

_____
_____
_____
_____
_____
_____
_____

XIV. FILL IN THE BLANKS > audio

Mike:　Linda good morning

Linda:　Hey Mike, what´s _____ ?

Mike:　Not much, just having a good time !!

Linda:　Mike I´m curious, are _____ from California?

Mike:　Well...yes, I am. Why?

Linda:　Because _____ are very similar to people from the east coast.

Mike:　I am?

Linda:　Yes, _____ are.

Mike:　So???

Linda:　Mmm...nothing...It´s just....funny, different.

Mike:　And what about you?

Linda:　What about me?

Mike:　Are you really from Boston?

Linda:　Of course I _____ !! Why do you ask?

Mike:　Because you are so typical of people from California.

Linda:　I am?

Mike:　Oh my God Linda. You definitely are.

Linda:　Name 3 reasons why _____ am please.

Mike:　OK. Number 1, you are very dynamic. Number 2, you are so tanned.....

Linda:　Haaaa !!!

Mike:　And number 3, you speak sooooo Californian.

Linda:　Ughh. But I am a Bostonian remember.

Mike:　Yes, with a Californian accent. Haaa .

Linda:　Mike, can I ask you a few questions and get a completely honest answer?

Mike:　Of course !!

Linda:　Please _____ very direct.

Mike:　No problem, you are sooo, mysterious.

Linda:　OK, here we go. First question.

13

Mike: Wait, wait… Linda. Why are you asking me these questions?
Linda: Mike, just answer will ya? _____ you honest?
Mike: I am.
Linda: Second question: Are _____ dynamic and responsible?
Mike: Of course I am.
Linda: Are you intelligent, professional and talented?
Mike: Linda !!!
Linda: _____ you…Mike?
Mike: I am totally professional and talented. And…I am intelligent too. Why?
Linda: Good Mike. Please finish your school project today. Professor Collins _____ very strict.
Mike: Linda, I know _____ is very strict.
Linda: You do?
Mike: I´ve heard rumors that he _____ a little…monster.
Linda: Really??? That's funny. I don´t think so.
Mike: And not only that, he is strict, inflexible, and explosive.
Linda: Explosive !!!! (angrily)
Mike: Linda, come on !!! Is his classroom afraid of him?
Linda: Mmmmm, a little.
Mike: Is _____ voice strong and commanding?
Linda: Of course his voice is strong and commanding; he is a teacher.
Mike: Is _____ face sometimes too serious?
Linda: Oh Mike, his _____ is serious because **he is** a serious man.
Mike: Why are you defending Professor Collins.
Linda: Because _____ friend Linda is Linda Collins.
Mike: Linda Collins?? You mean Professor Collins is…..
Linda: Yes, Mike. Professor Collins _____ my father.
Mike: _____ father !!
Linda: Yes, Michael Stevens. Professor Collins **is** my father.
Mike: Well, I really appreciate _____ father, he is a very professional man.
Linda: Michael, say goodbye to Linda Collins.

XV. POWERHOUSE audio

Hi this _____ Willie Jolley, and I _____ to welcome you to "It Only Takes A Minute To Change Your Life!" The _____ Motivation & Music Power Book. Music designed not _____ to help you shake _____, but to help you make it and take it to another level. I want _____ take you _____ a journey! A journey that _____ on the plains of the Serengetti, yet _____ a journey that begins every day… right where **you** live. Every morning in Africa, a gazelle _____ up and _____ that it must run faster than the fastest lion or it _____ be killed and eaten. Also every morning in Africa, a lion wakes up and knows that it _____ OUTRUN the _____ gazelle or it will starve to death.

It _____ not matter WHETHER you _____ a lion or a gazelle; when the sun comes up … you'd better ___ running. Folks it's time to get running! It's time to ___ going. It's time to get moving and _____ time to start flying, by trying and buying into your possibilities. It's time to live your dream! It _____ Takes A Minute, To Change Your Life! So _____ the journey begin, It Only Takes A Minute _____ Change Your Life!

Questions and answers:

Are you going to the <u>bank</u>?   Yes, I'm going to the <u>bank</u>.
Is Batman a <u>bad</u> hero?   No, Batman isn't a <u>bad</u> hero.
Are there <u>bats</u> at the zoo?   No, there aren't <u>bats</u> at the zoo.
Do you have a police <u>badge</u>?   No, I don't have a police <u>badge</u>.

Are there <u>balloons</u> in a party?   Yes, there are <u>balloons</u> in a party.
Do you need a <u>bat</u> for baseball?   Yes, I do.
Are there any groceries in the <u>bag</u>?   Yes, there are some groceries in the <u>bag</u>.
Is taking a <u>bath</u> relaxing?   Yes, taking a <u>bath</u> is relaxing.
What is this?   It's a <u>balloon</u>.
Where is your <u>back</u>?   It's the part of your body behind you.

REAL STORY

_____
_____
_____
_____
_____
_____
_____
_____
_____
_____
_____
_____
_____
_____
_____
_____
_____
_____
_____

LINK

_____
_____
_____
_____
_____
_____
_____
_____
_____
_____
_____
_____
_____
_____
_____

PREPOSITIONS

EITHER

THE HUNK
FOUNDATIONS 2. CHAPTER 2 (BE, PREPOSITIONS, EITHER)

I. VOCABULARY ▸ audio

1. Excited
2. Cute
3. Close to
4. Library
5. Send
6. Assignments
7. Streets
8. Files

( ) Ricky Martin is _____ for some girls. Babies are _____, too.
( ) When children go to Disneyland, they are very _____.
( ) A _____ is usually public and offers many books for people.
( ) The opposite of distant is _____. China is _____ Japan.
( ) The teachers give many _____ to their students.
( ) _____ in Guadalajara are very beautiful and clean.
( ) The secretary puts the digital information in electronic _____.
( ) I _____ the information via e-mail.

II. RHYMES

Flight	Right	Plight	Night
Glasses	Masses	Molasses	Passes
Purse	Nurse	Curse	Assures
Suitcase	Bookcase	Guitar case	Tool case

4- shelf wooden bookcase

Masses

III. TEXT ▸ audio

Linda: Susy, Susy !! I´m so excited, this guy is so cute.
Susy: Yayyy. Linda, what school is he in?
Linda: He´s in this school Susy.
Susy: He´s here, in this campus? What semester is he in?
Linda: In third semester, just like us. And he lives close to the Public Library.
Susy: The Public Library? Mmmm. Which Public Library, the one on 2nd Street behind the Police Station or the one on Orange Avenue inside the Park?
Linda: I don´t know Susy. Why do you ask?
Susy: Oh, never mind. Hey Linda we need to send our final assignment to Professor Thomson.
Linda: Is it complete?
Susy: Yes, I checked it with him and he says it´s OK.
Linda: I have the assignment on my computer, but I don´t remember which file it´s in.

Susy: *Is it* in the desktop?
Linda: Mmmmm. Nope.
Susy: What about in the school assignments folder?
Linda: Mmmmm. No, it´s not there either.
Susy: ***Which folder is it in*** Linda?
Linda: Let me see…..Oh I know, it´s in the "my school" file.
Susy: Ooops Linda sorry, it´s time to go. Time for my favorite show.
Linda: What channel is it on?
Susy: It´s on channel 26.
Linda: Ahhhh, 26 ¡!!! Just like Tom.
Susy: Yeah, just like Tom. Tom ????
Linda: Yeah Tom.
Susy: Which neighborhood does he live in?
Linda: In Aspen Grove homes in front of Rancho Santa Fe.
Susy: Oh yeah ??? And what street is his house on?
Linda: Why Susy?
Susy: Just tell me, will ya.
Linda: I think his house is on Sequoia Street.
Susy: Sequoia Street !!!! Tom !!! 26 !!! Linda….Tom is my boyfriend !!!
Linda: He is ???? Oh my god, I didn´t know….
Susy: Thomas Barrington, you´re gonna be veeery surprised !!!

Prepositions	
in	in the house
on	on the table
under	under the bed
next to	next to the refrigerator
behind	behind the curtains

IV. FOLLOW-UP QUESTIONS

- o   Is Tom Susy´s boyfriend?
- o   Is he courting Linda too?
- o   What street is his house on?
- o   And what neighborhood is his house in?

I. WRITE
Then repeat.

II. SPEED

III. PRACTICE

IV. SPEEDY VIDEO

V. MOVIE

_____
_____
_____
_____
_____
_____
_____

VI. LINK

_____
_____
_____
_____
_____
_____
_____

VII. REAL LIFE

_____
_____
_____
_____
_____
_____

VIII. PRACTICE IN PAIRS

- Are you IN the classroom?
- Am I IN FRONT OF you?
- Is _____ NEXT TO you?
- Is your book UNDER your hands?
- Are we IN FRONT OF each other?
- Is the lamp OVER us?
- Is the floor UNDER us?
- Are the pipelines BELOW us?
- Is Mexico BETWEEN Canada and the U.S?
- Is that wall BEHIND you?
- Is your book ON the table?
- Are the messages ON the board?
- Is the doorbell AT the entrance?
- Are the shoes UNDER the bed?
- Is the mother IN the kitchen?

I. WRITE
Then repeat.

II. SPEED

III. PRACTICE

IV. SPEEDY VIDEO

_____

_____

_____

V. PRACTICE IN PAIRS

1

- Is the yellow book on the chair? Yes,
- Which chair is it on?
- Are my keys on the table? Yes,
- Which end of the table are they on?
- Is my cell phone in my pocket? Yes,
- Which pocket is it in?
- Are my books next to the wall? Which wall are they on?
- Are the books on the table?
- Which table are they on?
- Is your teacher in a classroom?
- Which classroom is he in?

2

- Are you in a Spanish school? No,
- Which school are you in?
- Are we in the city of San Diego? No
- Which city are we in?

- Are we in the state of Sonora? No,
- Which state are we in?
- Are you a basketball fan? No,
- Which sport are you a fan of?
- Are we citizens of Canada? No,
- Which country are we citizens of?
- Are the books on the round table?
- Which table are they on?
- Are we in a Japanese school?
- What type of school are we in?
- Is she next to the teacher?
- Who is she next to?
- Is this material in unit 14?
- Which unit is it in?
- Is your house in front of a Starbuck´s?
- What is your house in front of?

VI. LINK

_____

_____

VII. MOVIE

_____
_____
_____
_____
_____
_____
_____

VIII. LINK

_____
_____
_____
_____
_____
_____
_____

IX. REAL LIFE

_____
_____
_____
_____
_____
_____
_____

X. PRACTICE IN PAIRS

- Are your mother and father in the state of Kentucky?
- Which state are they in?
- Is your boss employed in Coca Cola?
- Which company is he in?
- Is Santa Claus in Mex on the 4th of July holiday?
- Which holiday is he here on?
- Which state are your brothers and sisters in?
- Are we in a free country?
- What type of country are Iraqis in?
- Which pocket are your car keys in?

- Which bank is your account in?
- Which continent are Japan & China in?
- Which system is your stomach in, in the digestive or in the nervous?
- Which ocean are the Virgin Islands in?

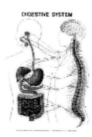

XI. FILL IN THE BLANKS  audio

Linda: Susy, Susy !! I´____ so excited, this guy is so cute.

Susy: Yayyy. Linda, what school is he ____?

Linda: He´____ in this school Susy.

Susy: He´s here, ____ this campus? What semester is ____ in?

Linda: In third semester, just like us. And he lives close ____ the Public Library.

Susy: The Public Library? Mmmm. Which Public Library, the one____ 2nd Street or the one on Orange Avenue?

Linda: I don´t know Susy. Why do you ask?

Susy: Oh, never mind. Hey Linda we need to send our final assignment to Professor Thomson.

Linda: Is it complete?

Susy: Yes, I checked it with him and he says it´s OK.

Linda: I have the assignment in my PC, but I don´t remember which file ____ in.

Susy: Is it in the desktop?

Linda: Mmmmm. Nope.

Susy: What about in the school assignments folder?

Linda: Mmmmm. No, it´s not there either.

Susy: Which folder is it ____ Linda?

Linda: Let me see.....Oh I know, it´s in the "my school" file.

Susy: Ooops Linda sorry, it´s time to go. Time for my favorite show.

Linda: What channel ____ it on?

Susy: It´s ____ channel 26.

Linda: Ahhhh, 26 ¡!!! Just like Tom.

Susy: Yeah, just like Tom. Tom ????

Linda: Yeah Tom !!!

Susy: Which neighborhood does he live ____?

Linda: In Aspen Grove Homes.

Susy: Oh yeah ¡!! And what street is ____ house on?

Linda: Why Susy?

Susy: Just tell me, will ya.

Linda: I think his ____ is on Sequoia Street

Susy: Sequoia Street !!!! Tom !!! 26 !!! Linda....Tom is ____ boyfriend !!!

Linda: He is ???? Oh my god, I didn´t know....

Susy: Thomas Barrington, ____ ´re gonna be veeery surprised !!

XII. G

on	in	next to
in front of	you	your house
in back of	he	neighborhood

XIII. ST

Describe your bedroom. **Example:. My bed is….I have a big lamp…. Use (In, on, next to etc)**

_____

_____

_____

_____

XIV. IE	+/-	So/Neither
My brother is in California.	but	and
My feet are in my shoes.	but	and
The Nile River is in Egypt.		
Alex and Tom are at the party.		
My hands are in my pocket.		
The cathedral is across from the City Hall.		
Snakes are in the desert.		
The Nile River is not in America.	but	and
Penguins are not in the desert.	but	and
The large intestine is in the body.	but	and
Birds aren't under the water.		
Africa is not in Asia.		
Michael Jackson isn't a Mexican artist.		
The respiratory system isn't in the abdomen.		

XV. MC
READ THE FOLLOWING AND YOUR TEACHER WILL TELL YOU.

Example:
Person A) Carl is a **26-year-old fireman** who lives in a 2-story apartment **near the beach**.
Person B) You told me **how old** Carl is, **what** he does for a living, and **where** he lives.

- Yosemite is in California, It is next to the Mohave desert. And it's a national park.
- Cancun is a nice place to live. It is in Quintana Roo. It is next to the state of Yucatan.
- San Diego is in southern Ca. It is in front of the Pacific Ocean. And next to Tijuana.

XVI. PRACTICE IN PAIRS
1
Are your feet in your shoes?
Yes, my feet are in my shoes.
Is your cell phone in your pocket?(bag)
Yes, my cell phone is in my pocket.(bag)
Is her new book next to her bag?
Yes, her new book is next to her bag.
Are the clouds in the sky?
Are your legs under the table?
Is the Jai alai across from Las Pulgas?

Are our eyes in our heads?
Are the brains in the cranium? Yes,

2
Are my keys in my left pocket?
Which pocket are they in?
Is the stomach in the nervous system?
Which system is it in?
Are you next to a Chinese student?
What kind of student are you next to?
Is the Nile River in Latin America?
Which continent is it in?

23

Are your personal photos in your business files?
Which files are they in?
Are the U.S. Virgin Islands in the Mediterranean?
Which part of the world are they in?
Is Sanborn´s across from the Caliente Race Track?
What´s it across from?

3

Are Trump and his wife in the White House?
Are we in the classroom or under the ceiling?
Are Baja California and Tijuana next to the Pacific Ocean?
Are baby kangaroos raised in or out of their mother´s pouches?
Is your vision clear and in color?
Are our books in Spanish or in English?
Are your birthplace and your hometown in the United States of Mexico?

Is your I.D. in your wallet? Yes,
Is Starbuck´s next to the Tijuana City Hall? No, ….. Wh…?
Are Tijuana and San Diego across from each other?
Are your parents in wedlock or out of wedlock?
Are The Beatles in the Hall of Fame? Yes,
Is Dracula in this city? No, wh…….
Are thoughts and words in your mind before they exit your mouth?
Are sea animals on land or in water?
Are cops under supervision?
Are Mexican Army soldiers out of control? No,
Are we living in a clean & safe environment?
Is contaminated water crystal clear and safe?
Is the brain inside the human body? Yes,
Are the clouds under the ground? No

4

XVII. PICTURE AND QUESTION
Listen to the audio and write the question. Then, practice the questions with a partner.

IN

_____   _____
_____   _____

ON

_____   _____
_____   _____

NEXT TO

_____   _____
_____   _____

XVIII. POWERHOUSE
Practice the questions on page 14, but using work examples.
Example: Which department is Steve in?   *WRITE 10 EXAMPLES*

_____
_____
_____
_____
_____
_____
_____
_____
_____
_____

H

1. helicopter helicóptero

Is a helicopter a big object?
Yes, _____.
Do helicopters fly very high?
Yes, _____.
Does a helicopter have wings?
No,_____.

2. hippopotamus hipopótamo

Is the hippopotamus a beautiful animal?
Yes, _____.

Are hippos very light animals?
No, _____.
Do hippos eat plants or meat?
Hippos _____.

3. history historia

Is history important in a person's life?
Yes, _____.
Does a person usually like history?
No, _____.
Do you like history?
Yes, _____.

4. Holland Holanda

Is Holland in Asia?
No,_____.
Is Holland in Europe?
Yes, _____.
Do you want to go to Holland?
Yes, _____.

5. honest honesto

Are you an honest person?
Yes, _____.
Are those people honest?
No, _____.
Do you want your children to be honest people?
Yes, _____.

6. honor honor

Is it an honor to be the president of Mexico?
Yes, _____.
Do people in jail deserve to be treated with honor?
No, _____.
Is she a woman of honor?
Yes, _____.

XIX. EITHER

Either has 5 applications:

1) To *propose or ask* 2 options.
2) To *deny* 2 options.
3) To say *any* of the 2 options is OK.
4) To say *None* of the 2 options.
5) The first one is "*no*" and the second one is *also* "no".

EXAMPLES:

1. To *propose or ask* 2 options.
   a. Are you *either* a student or a professional?
   b. Is your house *either* big or medium?
   c. Am I *either* here or there?

2. To *deny* 2 options.
   a. You´re not *either* a student or a professional. You´re a little baby.
   b. My house isn´t *either* big or medium. It´s small.
   c. I´m not *either* at work or at school. I´m home.

3. To say *any* of the 2 options is OK
   a. Would you like soup or salad? *Either* one is OK

b. Which car do you prefer, the Honda or the Toyota? *Either* car is fine.

c. *Either* of the 2 projects is OK. I don't mind.

4. To say *None* of the 2 options.

   a. Would you like soup or salad? I don't think I would like *Either* one. Sorry. Do you have quesadillas?

   b. Which car do you prefer, the Honda or the Toyota? I don't like *Either* car. I only drive Nissan. They are my favorite.

   c. I don't think *either* of the projects is recommended.

5. The first one is "*no*" and the second one is *also* "no".

   a. My father is not irresponsible and my mom is not irresponsible *either*.

   b. My company is not big and my car is not big *either*.

XX. "EITHER" EXERCISES

Please write 2 examples using the 5 different applications of EITHER.

1.
   a. _____

   b. _____

2.
   a. _____

   b. _____

3.
   a. _____

   b. _____

4.
   a. _____

   b. _____

5.
   a. _____

   b. _____

WRITE
Then repeat.

II. SPEED

XXI. REAL LIFE

XXII. EMAIL

XXIII. GUESS WHAT

The winner is the student who guesses the most questions.

1. What's something you have BETWEEN your ears?
2. Who's someone that lives NEXT to your house?
3. What are the ingredients people put IN their coffee?
4. What's something people sleep ON?
5. _____?
6. _____?
7. _____?

FROM

ADJECTIVES

MY HIGH SCHOOL BUDDIES
FOUNDATIONS 2 CHAPTER 3 (FROM, BE, ADJECTIVES)

I. WORD CHECK
Look up the meanings of the following words and write them on the blank space
- o Most _____
- o Look like _____
- o Each other _____
- o Instead _____
- o Move (home) _____

II. CONVERSATION 1

Ian: Hi, guys. What´s new?

All: Hi Ian.

Ian: Hey John, sorry but who are all these people?

John: They´re my friends from the trip.

Ian: The trip?

John: Yes, Ian. My trip to Europe.

Ian: And they all came from Europe?

John: Well.... Most did. Anyway, let me introduce you to my friends.

Ian: John, I...I have to go.. to ...

Mark: Hi Ian, I´m Mark. I´m John´s best friend

Ian: Best friend?

Mark: I´m from Germany.

Ian: Germany???

Mark: Yes, Ian from Germany. I know I don´t look like a typical German, but I **am** a German.

Ian: I didn´t say you....

Mark: Don´t worry Ian.

Ian: What about you?

Jake: What **about** me?

Ian: Are you Chinese?

Jake: No, Ian. I´m not a Chinese.

Ian: You´re not?

Jake: No, I´m not from China.

Ian: And where are you **from**?

Jake: I´m from Australia.

Ian: Wow, you sure don´t look like an Australian.

Jake: I know I don´t.

Ian: And you sure don´t speak like an Australian either.

Jake: I know that too Ian.

Ian: Tell me Jake…Which part of Australia are you from?

Jake: From Melbourne.

Mark: Melbourne? My parents are from Melbourne too.

Jake: Aren´t your parents German?

Mark: They´re Australian aborigenes, but they moved to Germany when they were little.

Ian: Ohhh, aborigenes !!!!

Mark: Yes, Ian aborigenes. What´s the problem?

Ian: Mark, I love aborigenes.

Mark: You do?

Ian: Yeah, I have an aboriginal last name.

Jake: What is it?

Ian: It´s Gorgotan.

John: What a strange last name.

Ian: And what is **your** last name?

John: You know it.

Ian: I know it, but maybe Mark and Jake don´t.

Mark: I know it, I know it !!!

John: Mark !!!!

Mark: Come one John. Don´t be silly. His last name is ….

John: Nooo, Mark.

Mark: John… His last name is Harrison.

J&I: Harrison???

Jake: And what is the problem with Harrison?

John: There´s no problem. But I don´t like it.

Jake: Well, now that we know each other´s names and nationalities, why don´t we have some lunch?

Ian: Yeah, let´s have some Mexican food, shall we?

All: Mexican??

Mark: Let´s have some tapas instead.

Jake: Tapas are Italian, right?

Ian: No, Jake. Tapas are from Spain.

Mark: Oh Jake !!! They´re Spanish.

John: Here we go again.

III. FOLLOW –UP QUESTIONS

- o Where´s Jake from?
- o Where are Mark´s parents from?

- o Are his parents aborigenes?
- o What´s John´s last name?

IV. INTRO

Adjectives	
Big	A big gorilla
Small	A small insect
Hot	A hot day
Cold	A cold beer
Intelligent	An intelligent student

Adjectives & colors	
Black	A big black gorilla
Yellow	A small yellow insect
Red	A hot red day
Amber	A cold amber beer
Black	An intelligent black student

V. PRACTICE

1
Is your name Anthony?
Yes, my name is ……
Are you from Cuba?
No, I am not from Cuba?
Where are you from?
Is she from Tijuana Baja California?
Yes, she is from Tijuana Baja California.

2
Is he from Carson City or is he from Tijuana?
He is from Tijuana.
Is she twenty two years old?
Yes, she is twenty two years old.
Is she ninety years old?
No, she is not ninety years old.
How old is she?
Are we from the United States of Mexico and are we Mexican?

3
Are they strangers or are they students?
They are students.
Is she very nice?
Yes, she is very nice.
Is she very problematic?
Am I nice and friendly?
Are we from good families?

Are we from dishonest families?
No, we are not from dishonest families.
What kind of families are we from?

4
Is your name Abraham Lincoln?
No, my name is not Abraham Lincoln.
What is your name?
Is your teacher short, fat and ugly?
No, he is not.
What is he like?
Is it hot in Alaska?
No, it is not hot in Alaska.
What is it like?
Are you sick today?
No, I am not sick today.
Are you blue today?
How are you today?
Is he unfriendly?
What´s he like?
Is Abraham Lincoln from Cuba?
No, Abraham Lincoln is not from Cuba.
Where is Abraham Lincoln from?
Are you from the Republic of Congo?
No, I am not from………
Which republic are you from?

VI. WRITE.
Then repeat.

VII. SPEED

VIII. OPPOSITES PART I.

_____   _____

_____   _____

_____   _____

_____

_____

IX. PRACTICE

X. OPPOSITES II

XI. PUT INTO ACTION

_____
_____
_____
_____
_____
_____

XII. MOVIE

_____
_____

XIII. MY CREATION

Write a question using the information on exercise IV. (Adjective + color + noun)

Adjectives & colors	

XIV. FILL IN THE BLANKS > audio

Ian: Hi, guys. What´s new?
All: Hi Ian.
Ian: Hey John, sorry but who _____ all these people?
John: They´re my friends from the trip.
Ian: The trip?
John: Yes, Ian. My trip to Europe.
Ian: And they all came from Europe?
John: Well.... Most did. Anyway, let me introduce _____ to my friends.
Ian: John, I...I have to go.. to ...
Mark: Hi Ian, I´m Mark. I´m John´s best friend.
Ian: Best friend?
Mark: I´m _____ Germany.
Ian: Germany???
Mark: Yes, Ian, from Germany. I know I don´t look _____ a typical German, but I **am** a German.
Ian: I didn´t say you....
Mark: Don´t worry Ian.
Ian: What about you?
Jake: What **about** me?
Ian: Are _____ Chinese?
Jake: No, Ian. I´m _____ a Chinese.
Ian: You´_____ not?
Jake: No, I´m not from China.
Ian: And _____ are you **from**?
Jake: I´m from Australia.
Ian: Wow, you sure _____´t look like an Australian.
Jake: I know I don´t.
Ian: And you sure don´t speak like _____ Australian either.
Jake: I know that too Ian.
Ian: Tell me Jake...Which part of Australia are you from?
Jake: From Melbourne.
Mark: Melbourne? My parents are from Melbourne too.
Jake: Aren´t your parents German?
Mark: They´re Australian aborigenes, but they moved to Germany when they were little.
Ian: Ohhh, aborigenes !!!!
Mark: Yes, Ian. Aborigenes. What´s _____ problem?

XV. DESCRIBING

XVI. POWERHOUSE

Describe two different family members in detail using the information you practiced on this chapter and present the information to a partner.

_____
_____
_____
_____
_____
_____
_____
_____
_____

Write 6 pairs of adjective + noun of terms used in your company.

_____   _____

_____   _____

_____   _____

XVII. OPPOSITES III

XVIII. GAME

Wearing,
Time,
Possessive
adjectives
&
Possessives names
sing and plural.

WHAT ARE YOU WEARING
FOUNDATIONS 2. CHAPTER 4
To be + Wearing, Time, possessive adjectives and possessives names (sing and plural)

I. PRACTICE 1

skirt | tights | boots | a pair of socks | hoodie
shirt | Pijamas | bow tie | dress | swimsuit
shorts | backpack | tie | trousers | bathrobe
T-shirt | jacket | Sweat suit | scarf | cowboy boots
sweatshirt | sweater | (business) suit | wallet | boots

II. MATCH

1. You look very good!   (   ) _____, yesterday I saw a guy stealing a car.
2. Oh come on Ian!   (   ) _____ why he didn´t pass the test.
3. All that stuff   (   ) Those clothes are very nice. _____
4. I do?   (   ) Dave: I think you play very well.   Tom: _____
5. Well, anyway.   (   ) In fact,_____
6. As I was saying.   (   )_____! Let me borrow your tablet!
7. No wonder.   (   ) Can you help me pick up _____.
8. Just… thinking.   (   ) They didn´t see us! _____
9. He's weird.   (   ) Mark: That´s a very nice watch.   Bob: _____
10. Just like yours, Mark. (   ) The break is finished. _____
11. I like your taste.   (   ) You know what I think about him? _____
12. Let´s go back to work. (   ) _____. I don´t like that kind of music.
13. That was sooo close.   (   ) Karen: What are you doing?   Pam: Nothing, _____

III. CONVERSATION 1   audio

Mark: Hi Mark how are you?
Ian: Fine Mr. Reynolds. How are you today? You look very good Mr. Reynolds
Mark: Oh come on Ian. I don´t say that !!
Ian: Yes, you do !! You always say, "Hi Mr. Reynolds, you look good, it´s a great
            day and all that stuff.
Mark: I do?
Ian: Yes, you do.

Mark:	Well anyway, as I was saying. Hi Ian.
Ian:	Hi Mr. Reynolds. That´s a very nice shirt !!
Mark:	Yes, Ian. I´m wearing a soft cotton shirt and also as you can see, I am wearing my gray suit.
Ian:	Yeah…. your gray suit. It´s your favorite, isn´t it?
Mark:	Well, no Ian, but it´s a strong color for a strong person.
Ian:	Yes, you´re right Mr. Reynolds. And why are you wearing a yellow tie?
Mark:	Yellow is the symbol of gold, power, abundance, Ian.
Ian:	Ohhh, no wonder.
Mark:	No wonder what Ian?
Ian:	Nothing, just ….thinking.
Mark:	Thinking??? Thinking what?
Ian:	I´m thinking that Mr. Reynolds is here.
Mark:	Mr. Reynolds is weird ?? Yes, he´s weird and I´m sure that right now he´s wearing his gray suit and his yellow tie.
Mr Reynolds:	Weird ???
Mark:	Excuse me?
Mr Reynolds:	Why are you saying I´m weird?
Mark:	Well….Mr….Reyy…..Mr. Reynolds, what I´m trying to say is that you are ….not typical. You are not a common person. You are…..unique.
Mr Reynolds:	I am?
Mark:	Yes, you are Mr. Reynolds. For example: you´re wearing a yellow tie and you´re also wearing a gray suit.
Mr Reynolds:	Just like yours Mark.
Ian:	Yeah Mark, just like yours.
Mr Reynolds:	I like your taste Mark. Well, what are we doing here? Let´s go back to work.
Ian:	Yes, Mr. Reynolds.
Mark:	Oh my God. That was sooo close.
Ian:	Hi Mr. Reynolds. Haaa haaa haaa

IV. FOLLOW UP QUESTIONS

1. Are Mark and Ian making fun of Mr. Reynolds?
2. What is Mark wearing?
3. Is that what he´s usually wearing to work?

V. WRITE.

Then repeat.

VI. SPEED

VII. PRACTICE 2

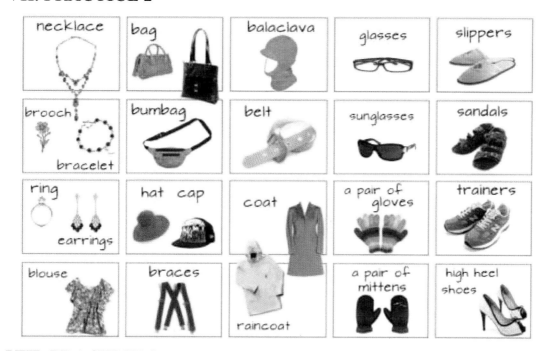

VIII. PRACTICE 3

Are you wearing a _____? Yes...
Is _____ wearing _____? Yes...
Are ____ and ____wearing ____? Yes...
Are you wearing ___because it´s ____?
Am I wearing _____? Yes...
Are we wearing _____? Yes
Am I wearing clean clothes? Yes...

RI-DI-CU-LOUS
ME-TI-CU-LOUS
FA-BU-LOUS
MAR-VE-LOUS
JEA-LOUS

Are you wearing extravagant clothes? No, I´m__
What type of clothes are you wearing? _____
Is _____ wearing a tuxedo? No...
What is _____ wearing?
Are you wearing pajamas right now? _____
What are you wearing? _____
Am I wearing ridiculous clothes? _____
What _am I_ wearing? _____
Is your boss wearing extremely elegant clothes?
What´s your boss wearing right now? _____
Is your favorite artist wearing old clothes now? __
What´s he/she wearing? _____
Are the children wearing soccer uniforms? _____
What are they wearing? _____

IX. OBJECT PRONOUNS AND POSSESSIVE ADJ.

I	Me	My	I love them.	This is my car.
You	You	Your	You love me.	This is your car.
He	Him	His	He loves us.	This is his car
She	Her	Her	She loves him.	This is her car.
They	Them	Their	They love her.	This is their car
We	Us	Our	We love them.	This is our car
It	It	Its	It loves me.	This is its car.

X. P2

1

Are these your things?
Yes, these are my things.
Are these the school's chairs?
Yes, these are the school's chairs.
Are these Claudia's books?
Yes, these are Claudia's books.
Am I the school's student?
Are we the building's occupants?
Are you one of Mexico's inhabitants?
Are we Mexico's power?

2

Are these Hitler's books?
Whose books are they?
Am I George Bush's teacher?
Whose teacher am I?
Are you Albert Einstein's student?
Whose student are you?
Are these bat man's chairs?
Whose chairs are they?
Is this superman's book?
Whose book is it?

4

Are these your belongings?
Are these my belongings?
Are these Maria's books and pencils?
Are these your chairs or my chairs?
Are these part of Claudia's property?
Are these part of the teacher's property?
Are these Maria's keys and coins?

3

ARE THESE MARIA'S KEYS OR MY KEYS?
AM I THIS SCHOOL'S INSTRUCTOR?
AM I YOUR NEIGHBOR'S INSTRUCTOR?
IS THIS MARIA'S CELLPHONE AND BOOK?
IS THIS CLAUDIA'S CELLPHONE OR MARIA'S?
ARE WE THIS CLASSROOM'S TENANTS?
ARE WE SPIDERMAN'S WORKERS?

5

ARE THESE YOUR CHAIRS AND TABLE?
ARE THESE YOUR BOOKS OR MY BOOKS?
ARE THESE YOUR BOOKS AND NOTEBOOKS?
IS THIS YOUR CELL PHONE OR MY CELL?
ARE THESE YOUR KEYS AND COINS?
IS THIS YOUR PENCIL OR MY PENCIL?
ARE THESE BACKPACKS YOURS?

6

IS MARIA'S JOB EASY? YES, MARIA'S JOB IS EASY.
ARE MARK'S FRIENDS SOCIABLE? YES, MARK'S .....
ARE ANTHONY'S FRIENDS AMIABLE? YES, ...
IS MARK'S JOB DIFFICULT? YES, MARK'S .....
IS ARNOLD'S EX-WIFE BEAUTIFUL? YES, ARNOLD'S
IS MICHAEL JACKSON'S MUSIC POPULAR? YES,
IS JUAN GABRIEL'S MUSIC RELAXING? YES,
IS JUAN GABRIEL'S MUSIC POPULAR? YES,
IS MARIA'S JOB EASY? YES, MARIA'S JOB IS EASY.
ARE YOUR TEACHER'S CLASSES DYNAMIC? YES,

7

IS KING KONG'S COAT WHITE? NO,
WHAT COLOR IS KING KONG'S COAT?
ARE THE LION'S CLAWS SHORT? NO,
HOW ARE LION'S CLAWS?
IS MARC ANTHONY'S MUSIC BORING? NO,
HOW IS MARC ANTHONY'S MUSIC?
ARE ABRAHAM LINCOLN'S CLOTHES LIGHT BLUE? NO...
WHAT COLOR ARE ABRAHAM LINCOLN'S CLOTHES
IS MICHAEL JORDAN'S UNIFORM YELLOW & GREEN? NO
WHAT COLOR IS MICHAEL JORDAN'S UNIFORM?
IS BILL GATES' BANK ACCOUNT SMALL? NO....
WHAT SIZE IS BILL GATES' BANK ACCOUNT?
IS SANTA'S BEARD SHORT AND BROWN? NO...
HOW IS SANTA'S BEARD?

8

IS YOUR FATHER'S ATTITUDE GOOD OR BAD?
IS ANTHONY'S BEHAVIOR UNDESIRABLE OR
UNWANTED?
WHAT ARE THE COMPANY'S BEHAVIORS?
IS ERIC'S CAR A FERRARI AND ITALIAN?
ARE ARNOLD'S CHILDREN JAPANESE OR WHITE?
ARE BOB'S HAMBURGERS DELICIOUS AND TASTY?
ARE CARL'S BURGERS GREASY OR ARE THEY
HEALTHY?
IS MARIA'S COMPLEXION NICE AND SMOOTH? YES

XI. MOVIE

_____
_____
_____
_____
_____
_____
_____
_____
_____

IS ANTHONY´S JOB INTERESTING? YES....
IS ANTHONY´S JOB A CAKE WALK? NO.   WH..
IS MARK´S HAIR LONG AND THICK? NO.   WH...
IS MARK´S HAIR CURLY OR IS IT STRAIGHT?
IS LINDA´S HAIRDO CONTEMPORARY? YES....
IS ANTHONY´S HAIR STYLE OUTDATED ? NO.   WH..
IS MARK´S SKIN SCALY AND ROUGH? NO.   WH...
IS MARK´S VOICE WEIRD OR IS IT NORMAL?

IS MARK´S SKIN WEIRD OR IS IT NORMAL?
IS YOUR BEST FRIEND´S MUSIC RELAXING?
IS YOUR FRIEND´S MUSIC UNPOPULAR? NO.   WH
IS MICHAEL´S MUSIC POPULAR AND UPBEAT? YES...
IS MADONNA´S COMPLEXION DARK OR IS IT LIGHT?
IS MICHAEL´S ANCESTRY AFRO-AMERICAN? YES...
IS EMILIANO´S HERITAGE ANGLO? NO.   WH...

ARE MEXICANS´ HOMES SMALL? YES, MEXICANS´ HOMES ARE SMALL
ARE SOME GIRLS´ PARENTS EASYGOING?
ARE MOST KIDS´ TOYS EXPENSIVE?
ARE TEACHERS´ IDEAS POSITIVE?
ARE MOST MEXICANS´ APPETITES LARGE?
ARE MOST AMERICANS´ HOMES NICE?
ARE MOST POLITICIANS´ LIVES BUSY?

ARE MEN´S CLOTHES MADE OF PLASTIC?
WHAT ARE MEN´S CLOTHES MADE OF?
ARE WOMEN´S CLOTHES OUT OF FASHION?
HOW ARE WOMEN´S CLOTHES?
ARE CHILDREN´S CLOTHES DULL?
HOW ARE CHILDREN´S CLOTHES?
ARE TEACHERS´ UNIFORMS WHITE?
WHAT COLOR ARE TEACHERS´ UNIFORMS?
ARE BIRDS´ NESTS GIGANTIC?
HOW BIG ARE BIRDS´ NESTS ?
IS MEXICANS´ DIET LIQUID?
WHAT ARE MEXICANS´ DIETS LIKE ?
ARE MOST MEXICANS´ HOUSES LUXURIOUS?
HOW ARE MOST MEXICANS´ HOUSES?

ARE MEXICANS´ HOMES STANDARD AND SMALL?
ARE WOMEN´S CLOTHES IN FASHION OR ARE THEY OUT OF FASHION?
ARE KIDS´ TOYS INTERESTING AND EXPENSIVE?
ARE MEXICANS´ DIETS LOW-FAT OR SPICY?
ARE TEACHERS´ IDEAS INTERESTING AND EDUCATIONAL?
ARE BIRDS´ NESTS MADE OF CEMENT AND FIREPROOF?
ARE MOST AMERICANS´ HOMES NICE AND MODERN?

ARE MEXICANS´ HOMES COZY?
ARE MEXICANS´ HOMES FANCY?
ARE MEXICANS´ HOMES EXPENSIVE OR AFFORDABLE? ARE SOME GIRLS´ PARENTS STRICT?
ARE SOME GIRLS´ PARENTS VERY LENIENT?
IS THE CHILDREN´S DEPARTMENT INTERESTING?
ARE CHILDREN´S TOYS INEXPENSIVE?
ARE CHILDREN´S DENTISTS UNEDUCATED?
ARE SOME MEXICANS´ CUSTOMS OLD FASHIONED?
ARE PIGS´ CUSTOMS CLEAN AND HEALTHY?
ARE BIRDS´ FEATHERS HEAVY OR LIGHT?
ARE MOST WORKERS´ IDEAS PRODUCTIVE?
ARE POLICEMEN´S UNIFORMS YELLOW?

EASYGOING

XII. TIME
Time, hours

10:00			
		9:30	
		12:00 pm	
12:00 am			

XIII. PRACTICE
Is it _____ am/pm? Yes it´s _____am/pm.   What time is it?

XIV. P2
Is _____am/pm the time when you´re at work? Yes, _____
Is _____am/pm the time when your boss is in the office? Yes, _____

41

Is _____ am/pm the time when ....? _____
Is _____ am/pm the time when ....? _____
Is _____ am/pm the time when ....? _____
Is _____ am/pm the time when ....? _____

XV. WHOSE

A. WHOSE (read the examples)

Is the Telmex company yours?
Whose is it? It is Carlos Slim´s company

Whose ____ ***OBJECT*** ____ is this? It is _____ ´s.
Whose ____ ***OBJECTS*** ____ are these? They are _____ ´s.

XVI. SPEED

B. COMPLETE THE SENTENCES (Use the apostrophe)

○ Whose car is this ? This is _____ car.
○ Whose book is this? This is _____ book.
○ Whose ideas are they? They are _____ ideas.
○ Whose _____ is _____? _____ Miguel´s _____.
○ Whose _____? _____.
○ _____? It is the Mexicans´ oil.
○ Whose son is Miguel? Miguel is Lupita´s son.
○ Whose daughter is Diana? Carla is Maria Elena´s daughter.
○ Whose son/daughter are you? I am my parents´ son/daughter.
○ Whose son is Alejandro Fernandez? He is Vicente´s son.
○ Whose father is Vicente? Vicente is Alejandro´s father.
○ Whose friend is Thalia? Thalia is Paulina´s friend, right?
○ Whose husband is your father? My father is my mother´s husband
○ Whose wife is your mom? My mom is my father´s wife.
○ Whose sister/brother are you? I am _____´s sister/brother.
○ Whose responsibility is it to finish your activities in the company? It is my responsibility

XVII. PRACTICE

My, your, his, her, our, their

Is Shakira´s husband rich?
Is her husband famous?
Is her mother in paradise?
Is her voice feminine?
Is Obama´s wife a Mexican?
Is his wife famous?
Is his business important?
Is his life good?

1

Is Michelle Obama´s husband poor?
How is her husband?
Is her voice strong?
How is her voice?
Is Trump´s house small?
How is his house?
Is his house in Tijuana?
Where´s his house?
Is Lupita his wife?
Who is his wife?
Is she his friend too?
Is she his babies´ mom?

2

XVIII. FILL IN THE BLANKS audio

Mark: Hi Mark how _____ you?
Ian: Fine Mr. Reynolds. How are you today? You look very good Mr. Reynolds.
Mark: Oh come on Ian. _____ don´t say that !!
Ian: Yes, you do !! You always say, "Hi Mr. Reynolds, you look good, _____ a great day and all that stuff.
Mark: I do?
Ian: Yes, you do.
Mark: Well anyway, as I was _____. Hi Ian.
Ian: Hi Mr. Reynolds. That _____ a very nice shirt !!
Mark: Yes, Ian. I´m _____ a soft cotton shirt and also as you can see, I am wearing my gray suit.
Ian: Yeah…. your gray suit. _____ your favorite, isn´t it?
Mark: Well, no Ian, but it´s a strong color for a strong person.
Ian: Yes, you´re right Mr. Reynolds. And why are _____ wearing a yellow tie?
Mark: Yellow _____ the symbol of gold, power, abundance, Ian.
Ian: Ohhh, no wonder.
Mark: No wonder what Ian?
Ian: Nothing, just ….thinking.
Mark: Thinking??? _____ what?
Ian: I´m thinking that Mr. Reynolds _____ here.
Mark: Mr. Reynolds ___ weird ?? Yes, he´s weird and I´m sure that right now he´s wearing _____ gray suit and his yellow tie.
Mr Reynolds: Weird ???
Mark: Excuse me?
Mr Reynolds: Why _____ you saying I´m weird?
Mark: Well….Mr….Reyy…..Mr. Reynolds, what I´m saying is that _____ are ….not typical.
Mr Reynolds: I _____?
Mark: Yes, you are Mr. Reynolds. Listen: you´re _____ a yellow tie and you´re also
Mr Reynolds: Just like _____ Mark.
Ian: Yeah Mark, just like yours.
Mr Reynolds: I like _____ taste Mark. Well, what are we doing here? Let´s go back to work.
Ian: Yes, Mr. Reynolds.
Mark: Oh my God. That was sooo close.
Ian: Hi Mr. Reynolds. Haaa haaa haaa

GAME

_____
_____
_____
_____

RP

_____
_____
_____
_____

43

XIX. SPEEDY VIDEO

_____
_____
_____
_____
_____
_____
_____
_____
_____

XX. MOVIE

_____
_____
_____
_____
_____
_____
_____
_____
_____

XXI. LINK

_____
_____
_____
_____
_____

XXII. REAL LIFE

_____
_____
_____
_____
_____

PRESENT PROGRESSIVE

WHAT ARE YOU DOING?

FOUNDATIONS 2 CHAPTER 5 (Present progressive)

I. VOCABULARY >audio>

1. Guests   ( ) My list is ready. Only one of my _____ is not coming.
2. Visiting   ( ) My _____ includes eggs, ham and orange juice.
3. Parents   ( ) Right now I am _____ around 4:30 A.M.
4. Postcard   ( ) My _____ are visiting from Veracruz.
5. Coming back ( ) I usually go to sleep around _____.
6. Midnight   ( ) This summer I am _____ Europe.
7. Getting up   ( ) Don't worry I will send you a _____ when I am there.
8. Breakfast   ( ) I'm leaving tomorrow, but I am _____ in 3 weeks.

II. RHYMES

Guest	Rest	Chest	Zest
Night	White	Kite	Flight
Postcard	Host	Ghost	Roast
Invite	Bright	Light	Bite
Listen	Prison	Risen	Is in
Breakfast	Fist	Missed	List

III. WORD CHECK

Look up the meanings of the following words and write them on the blank space

A) Surgery   _____
B) Veggie   _____
C) Healthy   _____

IV. TEXT

- Hi Doctor Daniels !
  - o Hi Dr Rogers. How are you guys? We´re just fine. We´re at the cafeteria .
- What are you guys doing?
  - o We´re talking about the surgeries of the day.
- Oh !!! Are you having lunch also?
  - o Yeah. That too.
- Are you having that lovely veggie mix (haha) ?
  - o Yeah, we´re having carrots, lettuce, tomatoes.
- Oh shocks, I´m eating a burger and you guys are eating so healthy.
  - o We sure are. (haha) Dr. Collins that´s a very interesting X-Ray
- I´m impressed Dr Rogers. You sure are motivating your team and giving them a good example of leadership and integrity.
  - o Thank you Doctor Daniels. I´m doing this because I believe this is very important for the hospital. So Doctor Daniels, which part of the hospital are you in now?
- I´m in the right wing.
  - o Oh that´s very nice.
- The right wing ??? That´s the part we´re in right now.
  - o Hi Dr. Rogers.
- Oh, hi Dr. Daniels.
  - o So….. Can I have some of that healthy food you´re having and watch that interesting X-Ray you´re discussing doctors?
- Well… sure… I guess

V. FOLLOW –UP QUESTIONS

- o Is Doctor Rogers watching a video or talking about the surgeries of the day?
- o What are they having for lunch?
- o Is he giving a good example to his team?

VI. P1

At this moment..	
I´m	speakING English
You´re	practicING your English
We´re	chattING in English
He´s/She´s/It´s	expressING ideas.
They´re	thinkING in English

VII. SPEED

VIII. PRACTICE

A.

1. Is that lady waiting for the bus?
2. Is Barack Obama achieving some of his goals?
3. Are you studying English right now?
4. Is the teacher speaking English?
5. Is your mom making spaghetti right now?
6. Is your boss pressing you to work harder?
7. Are the cars passing by very fast?

B.

1. Are the students and the teacher speaking Spanish in the class?
   What language are they speaking?
2. Is the president visiting Tijuana today?
   Where is he now?
3. Is the Mexican economy doing pretty well nowadays?
   How is the economy doing?
4. Is it raining now?
   How many people are using an umbrella right now?
5. Are the students reading a magazine?
   What are the students reading?
6. Is that airplane flying to Madrid?
   Where is that plane flying to?
7. Is the teacher writing on the board?
   What is the teacher doing?

C.
1. Are you sitting or standing?
2. Is the airplane flying or sailing?
3. Are the Obamas living in San Diego or in Washington, D.C.?
4. Are most streets in Tijuana being repaired or not?
5. Are the students paying attention to the class or are they sleeping?
6. Are the investors waiting for the economy to pick up or are they already investing their money?
7. Is the price of gas in S.D. increasing or decreasing?

D.
1. What time is the plane leaving?
2. Where is that taxi going?
3. Who are you practicing your English with?
4. What is your classmate drinking?
5. Are you watching TV or are you studying English now?
6. Is the City Mayor working or relaxing at this moment?
7. Are the police forces doing a good job or a "so-so" one?
8. Is President Obama planning to give the banks more help or not?
9. How much money is he planning to spend on financial aid?
10. Who is speaking English right now?
11. What is your classmate wearing today?
12. When are you taking a vacation?
13. Where are you going after class?
14. Is your shirt or blouse missing a button?

IX. WORD CHECK
Look up the meanings of the following words and write them on the blank space.
   A) Exploits   _____
   B) A major
      (in school)   _____
   C) Graduate school   _____

X. MY QUESTIONS
Write 3 questions for a partner using present progressive.

_____
_____
_____

XI. CONVERSATION 2 audio

Interviewer:	So what are your academic, or your professional exploits?
Student:	I´m a business major right now. So I´m hoping to…get my……graduate with a B.A. in Accounting and Business Administration. And then, after I go and get my MBA. I'm actually looking into getting my MBA JD, after I graduate.
Interviewer:	So, you want to go to graduate school here?
Student:	Here, UCR?. That's one of my options, but I'm actually looking other places in California, because going out of state, it´s really hard to go out of state.
Interviewer:	Have you considered Stanford? Have you ever considered that?

48

Student: I don´t know if…. You see, I don´t know if I have the best grades for that. Because it's a very competitive school. But, I think if I work at it, I might have a chance at it. But I know it´s such a great school to go to.

XIIFOLLOW –UP QUESTIONS

- o What´s the student hoping to do academically? He´s hoping to…..
- o What kind of master´s degree is he looking into?
- o Where is he looking to study these degrees?

XIII. R.P.

PERSON A You are Vicente Fernández; complete the following sentences about your life.

I'm running in my _____. I ride my _____. I'm preparing my song for this Friday's _____. I'm training my _____. I'm taking a plane to _____. I'm buying a new _____. I'm calling my _____ on the phone. I'm drinking a cold bottle of _____. I'm making a new music _____. My son is helping me with my new _____. We are participating in a new_____. We are taking care of our _____. I'm playing with my _____ I'm _____ the Cheyenne.

PERSON B   Ask Vicente Fernández some questions about his activities using
WHAT/WHERE/WHEN/WHY/WHO/ HOW + _____ing
Example: Why are you riding your horse Vicente?

G

LIVING	GOING	READING
DOING	WORKING	EATING
WATCHING	WALKING	WEARING

XIV. READING

Spanish	Simple present	Pres. Progressive	Future with __ing
Abrir	Open	I´m opening	I´m opening tomorrow
Agarrar	Take	I´m taking	I´m taking tomorrow
Aprender	Learn	I´m learning	I´m learning tomorrow
Beber	Drink	I´m drinking	I´m drinking tomorrow
Cambiar	Change	I´m changing	I´m changing tomorrow
Cerrar	Close	I´m closing	I´m closing tomorrow
Cocinar	Cook	I´m cooking	I´m cooking tomorrow
Comer	Eat	I´m eating	I´m eating tomorrow
Comprar	Buy	I´m buying	I´m buying tomorrow
Contar	Count	I´m counting	I´m counting tomorrow
Correr	Run	I´m running	I´m running tomorrow
Dar	Give	I´m giving	I´m giving tomorrow
Decir	Say	I´m saying	I´m saying tomorrow
Decir	Tell	I´m telling	I´m telling tomorrow
Despertar	Wake	I´m waking	I´m waking tomorrow

I'am walking
or
Sunshine

XV. READY FOR ACTION.

XIX. SPEEDY VIDEO

_____
_____
_____
_____
_____
_____
_____
_____
_____

XX. MOVIE

_____
_____
_____
_____
_____
_____
_____
_____
_____
_____

XXI. LINK

_____
_____
_____
_____
_____

XXII. REAL LIFE

_____
_____
_____
_____
_____
_____

XXII. IE	+/-	So/Neither
I am practicing my English	but	and
You're drinking some coffee.	but	and
I am doing my homework		
We're living in Tijuana.		
Mark's working in an office.		
My mom's cooking dinner.		
Maria's watching TV.		
Mike is not playing ball	but	and
Gloria isn't living in Las Vegas	but	and
Mrs. Brown isn't cooking	but	and
Mr. Taylor isn't driving a truck		
Sam is not walking home		
The concert isn't ending.		
The bus is not going downtown.		

XXIII. GRAND FINALE

2016

PREPOSITIONS II

DO
DOES

LOVER BOY
FOUNDATIONS 2 Chapter 6 (Prepositions II / Do, Does)

SPANISH	BASIC Infinitive	SIMPLE PRESENT I, you they, we	SIMLE PRESENT He, she it
Abrir	Open		
Agarrar	Take		
Aprender	Learn		
Beber	Drink		
Cambiar	Change		
Cerrar	Close		
Cocinar	Cook		
Comer	Eat		
Comprar	Buy		
Contar	Count		
Correr	Run		
Dar	Give		
Decir	Say		
Decir	Tell		
Despertar	Wake		
Dormir	Sleep		
Empezar	Start		
Encontrar	Find		
Entender	Understand		
Enviar	Send		
Escribir	Write		
Escuchar	Listen		
Esperar	Wait		
Explicar	Explain		
Ganar	Win		
Gastar	Spend		
Hablar	Speak		
Hacer	Do		
Hacer	Make		
Ir	Go		
Irse	Leave		
Jugar	Play		
Leer	Read		
Manejar	Drive		
Necesitar	Need		
Observar/ver	Watch		
Obtener	Get		
Oír	Hear		
Oler	Smell		
Olvidar	Forget		
Pagar	Pay		
Pedir/Preguntar	Ask for / Ask		
Pensar	Think		
Permitir	Let		
Poner	Put		
Querer	Want		
Reir	Laugh		
Romper	Break		
Saber	Know		
Sentir	Feel		

PART II

SPANISH	BASIC Infinitive	SIMPLE PRESENT I, you they, we	SIMLE PRESENT He, she it
Abrir	Open		
Agarrar	Take		
Aprender	Learn		
Beber	Drink		
Cambiar	Change		
Cerrar	Close		
Cocinar	Cook		
Comer	Eat		
Comprar	Buy		
Contar	Count		
Correr	Run		
Dar	Give		
Decir	Say		
Decir	Tell		
Despertar	Wake		
Dormir	Sleep		
Empezar	Start		
Encontrar	Find		
Entender	Understand		
Enviar	Send		
Escribir	Write		
Escuchar	Listen		
Esperar	Wait		
Explicar	Explain		
Ganar	Win		
Gastar	Spend		
Hablar	Speak		
Hacer	Do		
Hacer	Make		
Ir	Go		
Irse	Leave		
Jugar	Play		
Leer	Read		
Manejar	Drive		
Necesitar	Need		
Observar/ver	Watch		
Obtener	Get		
Oír	Hear		
Oler	Smell		
Olvidar	Forget		
Pagar	Pay		
Pedir/Preguntar	Ask for / Ask		
Pensar	Think		
Permitir	Let		
Poner	Put		
Querer	Want		
Reir	Laugh		
Romper	Break		
Saber	Know		
Sentir	Feel		

III. SPEEDY VIDEO

_____
_____
_____
_____
_____
_____
_____
_____
_____

IV. MOVIE

_____
_____
_____
_____
_____
_____
_____
_____
_____

V. VOCABULARY

1. Come on   ( ) Vamos anda cuéntame.
2. What's she like   ( ) Como es?
3. Trust   ( ) Puedes confiar en mí.
4. Political sciences major   ( ) Se va a graduar en ciencias políticas.
5. Slim   ( ) Mi vecina es delgada.
6. Bet   ( ) Te apuesto lo que quieras
7. Fool   ( ) A veces me comporto como un tonto (a).
8. Hang around   ( ) Quédate un rato mas, no te vayas.
9. Corny   ( ) Mi amigo el cursi.
10. Let's get going   ( ) Vamonos.
11. Threatening   ( ) Mi papá tiene una cara amenazante.

VI. RHYMES
Find words that rhyme with the words on the left.

Breakfast	A chest	My chest (body)	In jest
Station	Occasion	Vacation	Relation
Again	Pen	Hen	Den
O-fficer	**O**ffice	**Coo**perate	**O**peration
Rooster	Booster	---	---

56

VII. CONVERSATION

Ben: Ahhhh. ...She´s so pretty.

Jack: What are you saying Ben?

Ben: Me? Nothing. Why?

Jack: I heard you saying something about.....Sandy???

Ben: Sandy??? Sandy who?

Jack: Sandy Johnson.. You know who I´m talking about lover boy.

Ben: Come on Jack, I´m not telling anyone.

Jack: What´s she like?

Ben: Sandy?

Jack: Yes, Sandy you love bird.

Ben: Do you promise you´re keeping the secret?

Jack: Of course Ben. You´re my friend.

Ben: Are you absolutely sure I can trust you?

Jack: Ahh, never mind !!

Ben: OK Jack. She´s pretty and slim and feminine and she speaks 3 languages and she practices gymnastics.

Jack: Gymnastics. Wow !!! And what else does she do?

Ben: She helps a small group of children with disabilities twice a week.

Jack: Oh my… she sure does a lot of nice things.

Ben: You bet she does. And that´s not all. She´s studying political sciences and she wants to become an influential activist.

Jack: How old is she?

Ben: Sandy? She´s just 19.

Jack: Oh my goodness !! Does she have any sisters?

Ben: No, my friend. She doesn´t. But she has a brother.

Jack: Oh come on you fool. Or a friend, maybe she hangs around with similar girls.

Ben: Maybe she does. I´ll ask her.

Jack: Yeah, and we can go out and double date.

Ben: How corny Jack !!

Jack: Corny??? Look who´s talking.

Ben: Haaa. Just be patient and give me a couple of days.

A COUPLE OF DAYS LATER

Ben: Hey Jack, remember you asked about a friend of Sandy´s who had similar interests?

Jack: Yeah !!!! Is she here?

Ben: Yeah, she´s also multilingual, she´s also a political sciences major, she also helps little kids.

Jack: Where is she, where is she?

Ben: She´s right here !!!

Gunta: Hi Jack, my name is Gunta. Ben´s told me so much about you.

Ben: Well .. What are we waiting for ? Let´s get going !!!

JACK LOOKS AT BEN IN A THREATENING WAY BECAUSE OF GUNTA´S UGLINESS

VIII. FOLLOW –UP QUESTIONS

What´s Sandy like?

What are the attributes that Ben admires in Sandy?

Is Jack lucky with girls?

_____?

_____?

IX. SPEED

X. P2

1

Does your house have a kitchen?
Yes, my house has kitchen
Do the president and his family live in Los Pinos?
Does the place where you live have a garden?
Do most Mexican houses have a bathroom indoors?
Do most Mexican houses have running water?
Does the Marriot Hotel have a lot of rooms?

2

Do you like living in a very small place?
Where do you like living?
Does your house have ten bedrooms?
How many bedrooms does your house have?
Do you live alone?
Who do you live with?
Do most houses today have balconies?
What do they have?
Does your house have a laundry room?
Where do you do the laundry?
Do you have a grandfather clock?
What kind of clock do you have?

3

Do you live in a house or in an apartment?

Does your house have a garage or a parking space?
Do you like big houses or small ones?
Do you cook on a stove or in a microwave oven?
Do you keep ice cream in the freezer or the stove?
Do people sleep in the living room or in the bedroom?
Do you eat pizza at Joselito´s Pizza or at Pizza Hut?
Do Mexicans live in houses or in huts?

4

Is your house new or old?
How many rooms does your house have?
Do you live in a nice or in an ugly neighborhood?
Do you have a beach house?
Do you have a big stove?
Does the school have a kitchen?
How many rooms does the school have?
In which room do people eat?
Where do people sleep?
Do you usually sleep in the living room?
On what occasions do you sleep on the sofa?
Do Americans live in big houses?
Is it practical to live in a small apartment?

XI. AUDIO ▶ audio

Read conversation on page 43 one more time. Then, listen to the audio again.

XII. FILL IN THE BLANKS

IS, ARE, AM, DO, DOES			ANSWER		
	I	speaking English with you?	Yes,		
	Mary speak English or Spanish?		Mary		English.

Do		live in Chicago?		Yes,		
	your coworkers			Yes,		
Is		happy?		Yes,		
Is	Rebecca			Yes,		
Does	Rebecca			Yes,	she	

XIII. LINK

_____
_____
_____
_____
_____
_____

XIV. REAL LIFE

_____
_____
_____
_____
_____

XV. TELL ME ABOUT IT !!!

XVI. LISTEN AND REPEAT

XVII. WRITE I

XVIII. POWERHOUSE
Write an email to a friend.

To: _____

Subject: _____

_____
_____
_____
_____
_____
_____

XIX. GAME 1

XIX. GAME 2

XXII. IE	+/-	So/Neither
Do you get up early every day? Yes....	but	and
Do most people get up late on Sundays?	but	and
Do you have breakfast at 8 o´clock?		
Do big cars use up a lot of fuel?		
Does Shakira sing beautifully?		
Do you go out on weekends?		
Do you and friends work on weekdays?		
Do big cars use up a lot of fuel?	but	and
Does Shakira sing beautifully?	but	and
Do you and friends work on weekdays?	but	and
Do you get up early every day? Yes....		

XXIII. BE INVESTIGATIVE

Create a "Wh.." question using "do or does" with the information in the negative sentence.
Example: **_Student A)_** My car doesn´t run. **_Student B_**) Why doesn´t the car run?

1. The show doesn´t start at 7. _____ ?
2. The ice cream doesn´t cost $1.99 _____ ?
3. The ice creams don´t cost $1.99 _____ ?
4. Cats don´t bark. _____ ?
5. The class doesn´t permit Spanish. _____ ?
6. The teacher doesn´t speak Spanish _____ ?
7. The student doesn´t arrive at 5:05 _____ ?

XXIV. POWERHOUSE

Discuss what your boss wants, needs and asks for that is vital to the company.

_____
_____
_____
_____

XXV. PREPOSITIONS

ON
Monday, Wednesday, Revolution Street, July 4th, Facebook, Twitter, Netflix,
IN
The morning, the evening, the afternoon, China, San Diego, July, 2020, summer, July of 2020
AT
School, 12:00pm, night, noon, midnight, work, home.

WARNING !!!!!
AT and IN are both used for places.
But AT is more general.

IN... is more specific

We are AT *Speed Idiomas*™
I am AT work
I am AT home

IN the classroom.
IN the office.
IN the kitchen.

XXVI. EXERCISE
Write a small story using IN, ON, AT

___
___
___
___

XVVII. READING

XXVII. MOVIE

___
___
___
___
___
___
___
___
___
___
___
___
___
___
___
___
___
___
___

IS THERE
ARE THERE

DOES + HAVE

63

GUESS ???
FOUNDATIONS 2 Chapter 7 (Is there/Are there / Does + have)

I. VOCABULARY audio

1. Guess	( ) _____ That´s the right answer!
2. Hint.	( ) _____ is an animal that gives milk.
3. Sharp horns.	( ) _____? Yes, a rabbit hops all the time.
4. A bull?	( ) I´m going to give you a __ that will help U in class.
5. You got it !!! 2	( )The cow uses its tail _____
6. The habit of wagging its tail.	( ) Is that _____? Yes, it is.
7. Does it bark?	( ) I _____ he´s a good teacher.
8. A cow?	( ) Does a giraffe have _____?
9. To scare flies away.	( ) A dog has _____
10. A very long neck.	( ) Bulls sometimes have _____
11. Brown spots?	( ) _____ is an animal that carries many things.
12. Winks at	( ) _____? Yes, my dog barks all day long.
13. I got it, I got it.	( ) My girlfriend sometimes _____ me.
14. Does it hop?	( ) Do you know the answer? Yes,_____
15. A bushy tail?	( ) Do rabbits have _____?
16. A donkey	( ) Giraffes have _____

II. RHYMES

Surprise	Mice	Pies	Guys
Though	Stew	Blue	Too
Lovely	Doubly	Bubbly	Wobbly
Cushions	Shins	Mince	Bins
Comfortable	COMFFFF	TRRRRR	BLLLLLL
Furniture	Culture	Vulture	Rapture
Candles	Handles	Sandals	Randall´s
We´re EEEEEE	**Peer EEEEEE**	**Near EEEEEE**	**Ear EEEEEE**
Were	Her	Lure	Purr
Sunny	Bunny	Honey	Money

Sandals   Handles   Lice

III. WORD CHECK
Look up the meanings of the following words and write them on the blank space

A) Hint _____

B) Horn _____

C) Wag _____

D) Spot _____

IV. CONVERSATION 1

Wendy: Alright … You have to guess which animal I´m describing and ask me just 3 to 4 questions. I´m just giving you one initial hint. Ready ?

Everyone: OK

Wendy: This animal has short but very sharp horns.

Jack: is it big and black?

Wendy: Ohh. Yes, it is.

Jack: Is it a bull?

Wendy: You got it !!! 2 points for Jack. OK next pick. This animal has the habit of wagging its tail.

Bruce: Does it bark?

Wendy: Nooo. Haaa. It doesn´t.

Bruce: It´s not a dog?

Wendy: No, my friend. Next question.

Carla: Is it a big animal?

Wendy: It sure is.

Carla: Does this animal have horns too?

Wendy: It does.

Carla: Is it a cow?

Wendy: 2 points for Carla !!!!

Jack: Hey.. the cow doesn´t wag its tail.

Bruce: It does. To scare flies away. But it does.

Jack: Ughh.

Carla: Ha ha. Jack doesn´t have the proper attitude.

Wendy: Well anyway. Next animal. This animal has long and skinny legs.

Bruce: Does it have a long neck too?

Wendy: Yes, Bruce. It has a very long neck. You´re good.

Bruce: Does it have brown spots?

Wendy: No, Bruce. It´s not a giraffe.

Carla: Does it have feathers?

Wendy: Yeyyy. It does.

Carla: is it a flamingo?

Wendy: 2 more points for Carla.

Jack: Hey it´s not fair. You´re helping her.

Bruce: No, she´s not.

Wendy: OK. Our final animal has big teeth and big ears. (WENDY WINKS AT THE CAMERA)

Jack: I got it, I got it. Does it hop?

Wendy: No.

Jack: Does it eat carrots?

Wendy: Noooo.

Jack: Does it have a bushy tail?

Wendy: Nooooooo, Jack. It´s not a rabbit.

Jack: What is it then?

Wendy: It´s a donkey (SHE SHOWS HIM A DONKEY´S PICTURE)

Everyone: Haaaaaaaaaa

FOLLOW –UP QUESTIONS

o   What´s a bull like?   What about a cow?   And a donkey?

V. WRITE.

VI. SPEED

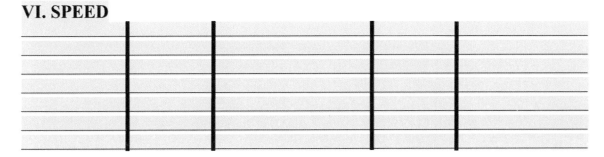

VII. INTRO

VERBS			
Do	I, you, they, we	have ?	
Does	He, she, it		

ANSWER		
Yes,	I, you, they, we	have .
Yes,	He, she, it	haSSSS.

VIII. PRACTICE

1

- o Do you have a bed in your room?
- o Does your dad work really hard?
- o Do your classmates study every day?
- o Does your boss yell when he is stressed?
- o Do birds sing when they are happy?
- o Do kids play with toys?
- o Does your mom cook really good food?

- o Do bathrooms have a television?
- o What do they have?
- o Do you have a pool and a jacuzzi in your back yard?
- o What do you have in your back yard?
- o Does your bedroom have a fireplace?
- o What does it have?

2

- o Is there a museum in the city?
- o Is there a coffee shop in every corner?
- o Is there a Soriana supermarket close to your house?
- o Is there a casino in this city?
- o Is there a big hospital in Otay?
- o Is there a cafeteria inside your company?
- o Is there a training classroom in your office?

3

- o Do you have a lion for a pet?
- o What do you have?
- o Do you have a plane?
- o What do you have?
- o Does your neighborhood have a gym?
- o Why doesn´t it?
- o Does your sister have a new car?
- o How old is her car?

4

- o Is there an Angeles Hospital two blocks from your house?
- o Where is the hospital?
- o Is there a day care next to your house?
- o Where is a day care?
- o Is there a karaoke club next to your house?
- o Where is a fun karaoke club?
- o Is there a movie theater in the middle of Arizona's desert?
- o Why isn't there a movie theater in the desert?
- o Is there a school next to your house?
- o Why isn't there a school next to your house?
- o Is there a Disneyland in Cuba?
- o Why isn´t there a Disneyland in Cuba?

IX. P1

Wh question + do/does				
What Where	Do	I, you, they, we	have ?	
When Why	Does	He, she, it		

Answer		
I, you, they, we	have .
He, she, it	haSSSS.

X. PRACTICE II

1

- Does your house have a pool and a soccer field?
- Does your room have windows and doors?
- Does your mom have long hair or short hair?
- Do houses have walls and roofs?
- Do people dance pop music or country?
- Do pools have water or ice?

2

- Does your house have 3 pools?
- How many pools does it have?
- Does your company have only lazy employees?
- What kind of employees does it have?
- Does your company have offices in the moon?
- Where does it have offices?

3

- Do cars _____ tires?
- Do rooms have beds?
- Do hospitals have _____?
- Do gardens have flowers and trees?
- Do factories _____ machines?

- Do _____ have marbles?
- Do you _____ medicines in your medicine cabinet?
- Do all _____ wear make-up?
- Do all boys play _____?
- Do kids play with _____ all the time or sometimes?
- Do artists _____ well?
- Do babies cry?
- Do Calimax supermarkets _____ beer?
- Do production workers _____ a uniform?
- Do _____ have teachers?

4

- Is there a mall in _____?
- Is there a _____ team in Tijuana?
- Is there a classroom in Philips?
- Is there a cafeteria inside Philips?
- Is there a _____ in the city?
- Is there a coffee shop _____ your job?
- Is there a park next to ____ house?
- Is there a television _____ your living room?
- Is there a church ___ your street?
- Is there a school close to your house?

XI. SPEEDY VIDEO

_____
_____
_____
_____
_____
_____
_____
_____

XII. MOVIE

_____
_____
_____

XIII. WRITE.

XIV. SPEED

XV. WHY.....?

XVI. WHY…..? PART II

WHY		MEXICANS		?
	DO			?
				?
	DO			?
				?
WHY				?
				?

XVII. PRICES

XVIII. HOLIDAYS?
Google the following questions. Then practice them with a partner.
https://www.whychristmas.com/cultures/

- When do Dutch celebrate Christmas?
- When do Japanese celebrate Christmas?
- When do Turks celebrate Christmas?
- When do Russians celebrate Christmas?
- When do Haitians celebrate Christmas?

XIX. CONTINENTS

_____   _____
_____   _____
_____   _____
_____

XX. LANGUAGES
GOOGLE   "LIST OF LANGUAGES BY THE NUMBER OF COUNTRIES IN WHICH THEY ARE
RECOGNIZED AS AN OFFICIAL LANGUAGE"

- **Where do people speak English?**

- **Where do people speak French?**

- **Where do people speak Arabic?**

XXI. DIFFERENT BREAKFASTS
Google   https://thepointsguy.com/2018/02/what-people-eat-for-breakfast-all-around-the-world/

- **What do Australians have for breakfast?** _____.

- **What do Chinese have for breakfast?** _____.

- **What do Filipinos have for breakfast?** _____.

- **What do Hindi have for breakfast?** _____.

- _____.

- _____.

XXII. MOVIE
_____
_____
_____
_____
_____
_____
_____
_____
_____
_____
_____
_____
_____
_____
_____
_____
_____
_____
_____
_____
_____
_____
_____
_____

HOMEWORK I
ANSWER THE FOLLOWING QUESTIONS

XIII. NEITHER
Neither has 3 applications:

1) To **deny** 2 options.
   a. Parker has neither slow employees, nor complacent employees.
2) To say **None** of the 2 options.
   a. Caterpillar can accept neither of those (2) bad behaviors.
3) The first one is "**no**" and the second one is **also** "no".
   a. Medtronic doesn´t tolerate indecision and neither does Greatbatch.

XIV. "NEITHER" EXERCISES
Please write 2 work-related examples using the 3 different applications of NEITHER.

1.
   a. _____
   _____
   b. _____
   _____

2.
   a. _____
   _____
   b. _____
   _____

3.
   a. _____
   _____
   b. _____
   _____

XV. SONGS 1* & 2*

1* In heavens name why are you walking away?
Hang on to your love.
In heavens name why do you play these games?
Hang on to your love.

Take time if you're down on luck.
It's so easy to walk out on love.
Take your time if the going gets tough.
It's so precious.

So if you want it to get stronger you'd better not let go.
You've got to hold on longer if you want you love to grow.
Got to stick together, hand in glove.
Hold on tight, don't fight.
Hang on to your love.

In heavens name why are you walking away?
Hang on to your love.
In heavens name why do you play these games?
Hang on to your love.

Be brave when the journey is rough,
It's not easy when you're in love.
Don't be ashamed when the going gets tough
It's not easy,
Don't give up.   *Sade ©*

2* You gotta keep kicking, you gotta keeping trying and you gotta keep believing in your dreams, and you've got to be committed.
Most people fail because they are not committed. Goethe said, "Until one is committed there is hesitancy, the chance to drawback, always ineffectiveness.

But the minute, the moment one definitely commits oneself, then Providence, the hand of God, moves also! Friends, whether it's professional or personal, whether it's in life, or in love … you gotta be committed.

Success in life takes a decision and commitment, and success in love takes a decision and commitment, because love is more than just an emotion, love is a decision. Someone said: "What's love got to do with it?" and I said, "everything!" Loves bears all things, believes all things, hopes all things, endures all things … love never fails. Love is more than just an emotion, love is a decision!

XVI. FILL IN THE BLANKS (has, does, have) & ANSWER.

A company _____ many different processes that require everyone's constant attention. What departments _____ your company have? _____ What important processes does your company _____? _____ A world-class company offers many different levels of quality that a typical smaller company doesn't _____. What are some levels of quality that your company _____? What doesn't your company _____? _____ What systems _____ your company have that maintain a high level of quality and service? _____ _____. Does Mexico have important companies that stimulate the economy? _____. What companies _____ Mexico have that represent an important part of the economy? _____
_____

JOBS

&

PROFESSIONS

WHAT DO I DO?
FOUNDATIONS 2 Chapter 8 (Does and do / Jobs)

I. VOCABULARY audio

1. Most	( ) The _____ is the person who cleans the bathroom.
2. During	( ) This office is _____ nothing will happen here.
3. Hurt	( ) I _____ at 4:30 in the morning and I get ready for work.
4. Sick	( ) I always play soccer _____ my lunch break.
5. Busy	( ) El Mexicano & The San Diego Tribune are _____ and have good _____ to read.
6. Through	( ) Mike Tyson _____ one of his opponents during a fight.
7. Midnight	( ) Business men are always really _____. They don't have time.
8. Hard	( ) I see my friends _____ week and on the weekends I never do.
9. Guard	( ) I need to _____ if we are working tomorrow.
10. Shift	( ) The grass was _____ with water this morning.
11. Dangerous/Safe	( ) Working the night _____ is very difficult.
12. Sprinkled	( ) There is a _____ at the entrance of every company.
13. Find out	( ) A fireman's job is _____ while a sweeper's is _____.
14. Papers/articles	( ) A new day comes right after _____.
15. Wake up	( ) _____ people work during the day.
16. Pretty safe	( ) The influenza will get you very _____.
17. Janitor	( ) A rock is always _____.

II. RHYMES

Lard   Wrinkled   Freckles

III. WORD CHECK
Look up the meanings of the following words and write them on the blank space

D) Handsome _____
E) How do you like? _____
F) Join _____
G) It´s settled _____

IV. CONVERSATION 1 audio

PETE: With so many options these days, I don´t know what career to choose Travis.
TRAVIS: I know. I feel the same way too.
PETE: The problem these days is that when I watch television, I prefer actors´ lifestyles.
TRAVIS: You´re such a fool Pete. An actor doesn´t really make that much money and you have no idea how difficult it is to get into that industry. An actor usually needs to be handsome and you, my friend are not....
PETE: I know, I know Travis. But there are some actors like...
TRAVIS: Like who?
PETE: Like..... Al Pacino. He´s not very handsome. And he makes lots of money.

TRAVIS:	OK Pete. Let´s be realistic. Let´s explore, just explore some alternative options, shall we?
PETE:	OK. What about, cage fighter? I´m strong, and I love that sport.
TRAVIS:	But you´re lazy buddy.
PETE:	So?
TRAVIS:	A cage fighter trains **really** hard.
PETE:	Yeah, I don´t like going to the gym, anyway. Maybe cage fighting is not a very good idea, huh?
TRAVIS:	How about ballet instructor? That means lots of pretty girls.
PETE:	A ballet instructor??? Come on !!! let´s get serious Pete. This is our future.
TRAVIS:	How does the word "judge" sound to you?
PETE:	Judge??? It sounds nice. Judge Peter Knowles presiding. All rise.
TRAVIS:	Holy Moly. It does.
PETE:	But how long does it take to be a judge?
TRAVIS:	Who cares how long it takes. It´s your future.
PETE:	Does your dad teach at Law School?.
TRAVIS:	He doesn´t teach **there**, but he does teach.
PETE:	Where **does** he teach?
TRAVIS:	He teaches at the Western School of Law.
PETE:	Travis, you say your dad is always home, right?.
TRAVIS:	Why do you ask?
PETE:	And you say that he takes vacations twice a year, right?.
TRAVIS:	I think he does.
PETE:	Does he have benefits?
TRAVIS:	I don´t know what benefits his company gives him, but he´s always smiling at home. He´s not constantly angry. So I think he likes his job. But Travis, you are a musician, aren´t you? You love music. You need to try going to music school, join a small band or orchestra and see how you like it. Don´t you think?
PETE:	Maybe you´re right. A musician always has fans and travels a lot and….
TRAVIS:	And you don´t have to wear a uniform, or a tie.
PETE:	And a really famous artist has a mansion in Miami or Beverly Hills.
TRAVIS:	Maybe I should be a musician too.
PETE:	Wow Travis. We can have a band. I´ll be the vocalist and you can play the drums..
TRAVIS:	Well, it´s settled. Music school it is.
PETE:	To our future Travis..

FOLLOW –UP QUESTIONS

* Why does Pete feel confused?

* Why doesn´t he want to be a cage fighter?

* Does the idea of being a judge sound good?

V. OCCUPATIONS 1

An accountant	protects a company´s finances
An engineer	optimizes resources
A designer	creates solutions
A manager	leads teams
A teacher	helps students learn new things
A supervisor	checks if people follow the rules
A scientist	does research and development.
A priest	gives mass on Sundays

OCCUPATIONS 2

1

2

3

4

5

6

WRITE THE NUMBER

(   )   Cuts fabrics, measures her customers' clothes and sews buttons.

(   ) Cuts her customers' hair, dyes some women's hair and suggests beauty products.

(   ) Cleans people's homes, sometimes prepares lunch and can even take kids to school and pick them up.

(   ) Puts out fires, helps old ladies to cross the street and rescues people in danger.

(   ) Controls the traffic, gives speeding tickets and pulls people over.

PRACTICE THE FOLLOWING

- Who stops people when they speed?
- Who uses chemicals to make their clients more sophisticated?
- Who carries hoses when a fire is out of control?
- Who uses scissors every day?
- Who blows a whistle?
- Who uses a rag, a mop & a broom?
- Who smiles when they give us an expensive coffee?

WHAT THEN

a) If a Barista doesn't design clothes, what does she do?
b) If a cop doesn't comb people's hair, what does he do?
c) If a hair stylist doesn't clean people's homes, what does she do?
d) If a maid doesn't serve coffees all day, what does she do?

OCCUPATIONS 3

XIV. SPEED

XIII. LINK

OCCUPATIONS 4

Average Entry-Level and Senior Software Developer Salaries in the World

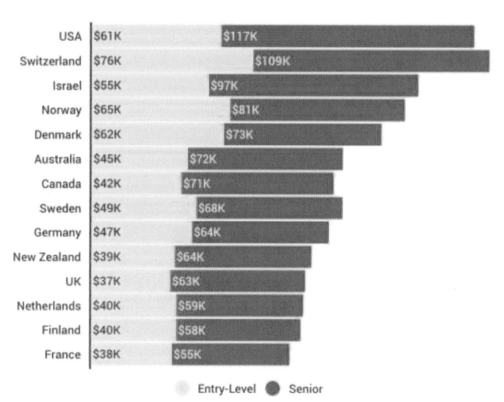

Entry-Level ● Senior

Source: daxx.com

PRACTICE

1

Do you live in this city?
Do you study English?
Do you go to church every Sunday?
Does your favorite artist live _____?
Does your brother live in México?
Does your dad play pool?
Does your mom go to church?

2

Do you work in a hospital?
What do you do?
Do you like swimming in the beach?
Where do you like to swim?
Do you sing in the shower?
Where do you sing?
Does your mom cook every day?
When does she cook?

3

Do you study during the week or on the weekends?

Do you have English class on Mondays and Wednesdays?
Do you exercise in the morning or at night?
Does your teacher live In this city or in another one?
Does your dog play Frisbee or catch?
Does your office have windows?

4

Do You Like Sports?
Do You Like _____?
Do you have a _____ ?
Do you go _____ every Saturday?
Do you want a new _____?
What do you do on the _____?
Where do you _____?
When do you go to _____?
What time do you _____?
Does your brother _____ with you?
Does your mom _____ for you?
Do you work _____ Saturdays?
Do you _____ every day?

VI. WORD CHECK

Look up the meanings of the following words and write them on the blank space

A) Folks   _____
B) Face (v)   _____
C) Climb   _____
D) Thoughts (n)   _____

VII. CONVERSATION 2

For the White House initiatives, including the White House Hispanic Initiative. When President Obama first came to office, a lot of folks knew that he´d just faced a hill of problems, there was a mountain of problems. And we started to climb, but there are still people who don´t know all of the different federal resources, the protections and the services we provide. And so one of my jobs is to make sure that we´re communicating that to the public. And especially the folks who need it the most right now. So I´d love to hear about your ideas and your thoughts about, how we can get that worked out. Thank you.

FOLLOW –UP QUESTIONS

○ Are there still people who don´t have information about the different government programs?
○ What does he need to make sure of?
○ Does he want to work with other people?

RP 1

Imagine You Interviewed a Famous Person, Tell Us About His/ Her Schedule. Example: He Exercises Every Day. He Goes To The Gym, Etc. Choose Someone You like.

RP 2

Imagine You Are A Movie Director, Tell Us About Your Daily Activities And Projects.

GAME

IE

+- Student 1	Student 2
I work every day.	I don´t
I study French.	We don´t
I do homework every day.	They don´t
I take the bus to come to class.	Jay doesn´t
I teach English	We don´t
I have two cats.	Rick doesn´t
I don´t work on weekends.	I do
I don´t study French.	We do
I don´t do dishes.	They do
I don´t watch T.V. at night.	Kids do
Lisa doesn´t cook.	Moms do
Ryan doesn´t exercise.	Girls do

SO/NEITHER

	Student 2
Diane works out.	So does Brian.
Brandon takes the bus.	So does Rosy
I do Pilates.	So do they
I have a new computer.	So do we
I see my sister every Sunday.	So does Ben
I clean my bedroom on Saturday	So do I
I don´t close my window at night.	Neither do I
I don´t eat meat.	Neither do we
Rebecca doesn´t have a car.	Neither does Carl.
Bob doesn´t clean his bedroom.	Neither does Brian
Erica doesn´t speak Spanish.	Neither does Lisa
I don´t watch T.V. every day.	Neither do they

MC

ANSWER FOLLOWING ONLY THIS PATTERN !!!
You told me what, where, when, why, who etc

Mariana Loves Pop Music _____
She Goes To School _____
She Wants To Be An Attorney _____
Luis Teaches English And French _____
He Was Born In The U.S. _____
He Likes To Exercise Every Day. _____
Alexander Works In An American Company _____
He Likes To Play The Violin. _____
Brittany Likes To Go To The Movies. _____
She Wants To Be A Movie Director. _____
She Is A Designer. _____

XI. OCCUPATIONS 2

Occupations	Listen, repeat and fill in the blanks.	
A security guard doesn´t	protect a company´s finances	
An import-export supervisor doesn´t	optimize resources inside the finance dept	
A teacher doesn´t	create solutions on software design	
A QA manager doesn´t	contact vendors	
A BU leader doesn´t	help students learn new things	
A line leader doesn´t	attend staff meetings	

XII. SONG

This may come, this may come as some surprise
But I miss you
I could see through all of your lies
But still I miss you

He takes her love, but it doesn't feel like mine
He tastes her kiss, her kisses are not wine, they're not mine
He takes, but surely she can't give what I'm feeling now
She takes, but surely she doesn't know how

Is it a crime
Is it a crime
That I still want you
And I want you to want me too

My love is wider, wider than Victoria Lake
My love is taller, taller than the Empire State
It dives, it jumps and it ripples like the deepest ocean

I can't give you more than that, surely you want me back

Is it a crime
Is it a crime
I still want you
And I want you to want me too

My love is wider, wider than Victoria Lake
My love is taller, Taller than the Empire State
It dives, it jumps
I can't give you more than that, surely you want me back
Is it a crime Is it a crime
That I still want you
And I want you to want me too
It dives, it jumps and it ripples like the deepest ocean
I can't give you more than that, surely you want me back
Tell me is it a crime

Sade ©

XIII. POWERHOUSE

Describe what´s the importance of 3 different positions in this company.
Example: ___*The production supervisor is very important because he ......*___

_____
_____
_____
_____
_____
_____
_____
_____

81

What are some dangerous jobs and why are they dangerous?

JOB   WHY

———————————   ——————————————————————

———————————   ——————————————————————

———————————   ——————————————————————

———————————   ——————————————————————

———————————   ——————————————————————

What are some jobs you would recommend to your children and why?

JOB   WHY

———————————   ——————————————————————

———————————   ——————————————————————

———————————   ——————————————————————

———————————   ——————————————————————

———————————   ——————————————————————

———————————   ——————————————————————

———————————   ——————————————————————

Describe and discuss what´s the power of this company´s system.

———

———

———

———

———

———

———

———

———

———

———

———

What are some NEW jobs that are very important in this economy and in the future?

JOB   WHY

———————————   ——————————————————————

———————————   ——————————————————————

———————————   ——————————————————————

———————————   ——————————————————————

———————————   ——————————————————————

COGNATES ENGLISH-SPANISH
Foundations 2

EXERCISE
Practice the following questions with a partner. **Take turns** and give **complete** answers.

H

1. hospital hospital

Is the hospital a nice place to be?
No, _____.
Are you happy to be in a hospital?
No, _____.
Do you like to visit people in the hospital?
Yes, _____.

2. hotel hotel

Is this the right hotel?
Yes, _____.
Are you going to stay in a Marriot hotel?
No, _____.
Do you stay in hotels or hostels?
I_____.

3. hour hora

Is it right now the rush hour?
Yes, _____.
Are you leaving from work in an hour?
No, _____.
Do you need that job in an hour?
Yes, _____.

4. human humano(a)

Is she a very kind and human person?
Yes, _____.
Is the dog expression almost human?
No, _____.
Do you read about human history?
Yes, _____.

I

1. idea idea

Is this a good idea?
Yes, _____.

Are those ideas reflecting the company's mission?
No, _____.
Do you think that idea is correct?
No, _____.

2. identification identificación

Is your identification real or a fake?
My _____.
Are you going to change your driver's ID?
No, _____.
Do you have the official IFE identification?
Yes, _____.

3. imagine (to) imaginar

Is it difficult to imagine?
Yes, _____.
Are they imagining terrible things?
No, _____.
Can you imagine a million of dollars?
Yes, _____.

4. immigrants inmigrantes

Is there a large immigrant population?
Yes, _____.
Are your neighbors immigrants from Italy?
No, _____.
Do you think immigrants are dangerous?
Yes, _____.

1. immediately inmediatamente

Is it important to bring it immediately?
Yes, _____.
Are you sure you want it immediately?
No, _____.
Can you give it to me immediately?

Yes, _____ .

2. importance importancia

Is this a matter of little importance?
Yes, _____ .
Are you sure of the importance of education?
No, _____ .
Are you concerned of the importance of values?
Yes, _____ .

3. important importante

Is it important to speak English?
Yes, _____ .
Is it important to speak Portuguese?
No, _____ .
Do you think money is important?
Yes, _____ .

4. impressed impresionando(a)

Is he impressed with the new secretary?
Yes, _____ .
Are you impressed with Avatar movie?
No, _____ .
Do you get impressed easily?
Yes, _____ .

5. impression impression

Was that a terrible impression?
Yes, _____ .
Are you having a good impression of me?
No, _____ .
Do you have a good impression of him?
Yes, _____ .

6. increase incrementar

Is it important to increase the price?
Yes, _____ .
Are the houses increasing in value?
No, _____ .
Do you increase the price of the English class?
Yes, _____ .

7. incredible increíble

Isn't that girl incredible?
Yes, _____ .
Are you the incredible Hulk?
No, _____ .
Do you believe in incredible things?
Yes, _____ .

8. incurable incurable

Is AIDS incurable?
Yes, _____ .
Is he having an incurable optimism?
Yes, _____ .
Do you have an incurable illness?
No, _____ .

9. independence independencia

Is it today Independence Day?
Yes, _____ .
Are you having financial independence?
No, _____ .
Do you celebrate Independence Day?
Yes, _____ .

10. information información

Is he looking for the correct information?
Yes, _____ .
Are you sure about that information?
No, _____ .
Do you give false information?
No, _____ .

11. insects insectos

Is that a dangerous insect?
Yes, _____ .
Are you allergic to insects?
No, _____ .
Do you really like insects?
Yes, _____ .

12. inseparable inseparable

Is this problem inseparable from the other?
Yes, _____ .
Are you and Tony inseparable friends?
Yes, _____ .
Is practice inseparable from learning a language?

Yes, _____.

13. insist (to) insistir

Is it really necessary to insist?
Yes, _____.
Are you determined to insist for another date?
No, _____.
Do you like to insist when they say no?
Yes, _____.

14. inspection inspección

Is that inspection really important?
Yes, _____.
Are you having an inspection again?
No, _____.
Do you make frequent inspections at your work?
Yes, _____.

15. intelligence inteligencia

Does she have an average intelligence?
Yes, _____.
Are they shining for their intelligence?
No, _____.
Do you know a person of superior intelligence?
Yes, _____.

16. intelligent inteligente

Is she very intelligent?
Yes, _____.
Are they really intelligent?
No, _____.
Do you like intelligent women?
Yes, _____.

17. interesting interesante

Is that TV show interesting?
Yes, _____.
Are they interesting people?
No, _____.
Do you read interesting books?
Yes, _____.

18. interrupt (to) interrumpir

Is William Levy interrupting the class?
Yes, _____.
Are my friends interrupting the lecture?
No, _____.
Do students interrupt the class constantly?
Yes, _____.

19. introduce (to) introducer

Is it important to introduce your girlfriend?
Yes, _____.
Are you introducing your parents?
No, _____.
Do you introduce your students?
Yes, _____.

20. introduction introducción

Is the introduction of the book interesting?
Yes, _____.
Is the introduction of the opera very impressive?
No, _____.
Is the introduction of the telephone service important?
Yes, _____.

21. invent (to) inventar

Is he inventing a long story?
Yes, _____.
Are you inventing those excuses?
No, _____.
Do you invent new substances?
Yes, _____.

22. investigate (to) investigar

Is he here to investigate the crime?
Yes, _____.
Is the investigation without a problem?
No, _____.
Do you investigate very well about your daughter's boyfriends?
Yes, _____.

23. invitation invitación

Is this a royal invitation for the dance?
Yes, _____.
Do they have an invitation to the party?
No, _____.

Do you want an invitation to Paulina's birthday party?
Yes, _____.

24. invite (to) invitar

Is she inviting her boyfriend?
Yes, _____.
Are you inviting your girlfriend?
No, _____.
Do you invite your in-laws to a vacation?
Yes, _____.

25. island isla

Is this a very big, beautiful island?
Yes, _____.
Are you going to "Tres Marias" island?
No, _____.
Do you swim at the island's beach?
Yes, _____.

L

1. leader líder

Is he the leader we need?
Yes, _____.
Are you willing to do all the new leader tasks?
No, _____.
Do you like the new company leader?
Yes, _____.

2. lemon limón

Is lemon sour or sweet?
It _____.
Are those lemons ripe already?
No, _____.
Do you squeeze lemon on most of your food?
Yes, _____.

3. lens lente

Is that lens adequate for the telescope?
Yes, _____.
Are those lenses yours?
No, _____.
Do you want to change the microscope lens?
Yes, _____.

4. leopard leopardo

Is the leopard a beautiful animal?
Yes, _____.
Are you willing to touch the leopard?
No, _____.
Do you like to fight with leopards?
Yes, _____.

5. lesson lección

Is that a good lesson for productivity?
Yes, _____.
Are you learning from that lesson?
No, _____.
Do you think that was a good lesson?
Yes, _____.

6. lessons lecciones

Are lessons 1 and 2 very difficult?
Yes, _____.
Are those lessons easy or hard?
They _____.
Do you need to practice lessons five and six?
Yes, _____.

7. line línea

Is that a curve or a straight line?
That is _____.
Are you working in the production line?
No, _____.
Do you work in line number 3 of the subway?
Yes, _____.

8. lion león

Is the lion a fierce animal?
Yes, _____.
Are lions big and beautiful animals?
No, _____.
Do lions live in Africa or Australia?
Yes, _____.

9. list lista

Is Jennifer on the guests' list?
Yes, _____.
Are you typing the lists the boss asked?
No, _____.

Do you make a list to go to the supermarket?
Yes, _____ .

10. locate (to) localizar

Is it difficult to locate her house?
Yes, _____ .
Are you trying to locate the new office?
No, _____ .
Can you locate that company easily?
Yes, _____ .

M

1. machine máquina

Is this a very good machine?
Yes, _____ .
Are those machines over there yours?
No, _____ .
Do you work with heavy machines?
Yes, _____ .

2. magic magia

Is Harry Potter a magic movie?
Yes, _____ .
Are they good magic tricks?
No, _____ .
Do you like to read magic books very often?
Yes, _____ .

3. magician mago

Is Harry Potter a magician?
Yes, _____ .
Are your mom and dad magicians?
No, _____ .
Do you think David Copperfield is a good magician?
Yes, _____ .

4. magnificent magnífico(a)

Was Titanic a magnificent movie?
Yes, _____ .
Are Everest & K2 magnificent mountains?
No, _____ .
Do you like the magnificent pyramids of Egypt?
Yes, _____ .

5. manner manera

Is that a good manner to treat your wife?
No, _____ .
Are those good manners to teach English?
No, _____ .
Do like the manner your husband treats you?
Yes, _____ .

6. map mapa

Is this the map we need?
Yes, _____ .
Are you checking the map for the trip?
No, _____ .
Do you have the company's map?
Yes, _____ .

7. March marzo

Is your birthday in March?
Yes, _____ .
Is she going to Argentina in March?
No, _____ .
Do you plan to go to Cancun in March or April?
I_____ .

8. march (to) marchar, caminar

Is she going to march in the next parade?
Yes, _____ .
Is the band marching onto the field?
No, _____ .
Do enemy troops march in the city?
Yes, _____ .

9. marionettes marionetas, títeres

Is a marionette something nice for a child?
Yes, _____ .
Are you able to handle marionettes?
No, _____ .
Do you like Marionette Theater?
Yes, _____ .

10. medal medulla

Is that a gold medal for your commitment to work excellently?
Yes, _____ .

Are you training very hard for an olympic gold medal?
Yes, _____.
Does she have a military medal for being at war?
Yes, _____.

11. memory memoria

Is this the result of your good memory?
Yes, _____.
Are you having memory problems?
No, _____.
Does she have a good memory?
Yes, _____.

12. metal metal

What is better gold or platinum?
I think _____.
Can you work with iron metal?
No, _____.
Does he make rings with iron or plastic?
He _____.

13. microscope microscopio

Is this a good microscope?
Yes, _____.
Are you happy with this new microscope?
No, _____.
Can you increase your productivity with this new microscope?
Yes, _____.

14. million millón

Is that car a million dollars?
Yes, _____.
Are you working in a $300-million company?
No, _____.
Does he have a million dollars in the bank?
Yes, _____.

15. miniature miniature

Is this a porcelain miniature?
Yes, _____.
Are those miniatures of the Petronas Towers?
No, _____.
Does she collect miniature cars?

Yes, _____.

16. minute minute

Is he coming in a minute?
Yes, _____.
Are they coming in five minutes?
No, _____.
I need to talk to you. Do you have a minute?
Yes, _____.

17. moment momento

Is this a good moment to talk with her?
Yes, _____.
Are they coming any moment?
No, _____.
Can you come to my office for a moment?
Yes, _____.

18. monument monument

Is that Abraham Lincoln's monument?
Yes, _____.
Are those girls next to Cuauhtémoc's monument?
No, _____.
Do you plan to sleep below Tijuana's monument?
Yes, _____.

19. much mucho

Is that too much sugar?
Yes, _____.
Are you drinking too much coffee?
No, _____.
Are you eating too much pizza?
Yes, _____.

20. music música

Is Mozart and Beethoven's good music?
Yes, _____.
Are you listening to Yanni's music?
No, _____.
Do you like Michael Jackson's music?
Yes, _____.

N

1. natural natural

Is this the Natural History Museum?
Yes, _____.
Are you using natural ingredients?
No, _____.
Do you make furniture with natural materials?
Yes, _____.

2. necessary necesario/a

Is the meeting really necessary?
Yes, _____.
Are you sure it is necessary to present the complaint?
No, _____.
Do you think snacks are necessary in the shopping list?
Yes, _____.

3. nectar néctar

Is nectar the drink Greek and Roman gods drank?
Yes, _____.
Is that mango nectar?
No, _____.
Do you like to drink fruit nectar?
Yes, _____.

4. nervous nervioso(a)

Is that girl over there a little nervous?
Yes, _____.
Are you nervous before an English test?
No, _____.
Do you get nervous when you have a new boss?
Yes, _____.

5. notice notar

Is he noticing his daughter's progress?
Yes, _____.
Are you able to notice any writing mistake?
No, _____.
Do you notice any change in the room?
Yes, _____.

O

1. obedient obediente

Is he an obedient son?
Yes, _____.
Are you an obedient employee?
No, _____.
Do you have obedient children?
Yes, _____.

2. object objeto

What is that object over there?
It _____.
Are those objects on the table yours?
No, _____.
Do you have any strange object in your car?
Yes, _____.

3. observatory observatorio

Is the San Pedro Martir Observatory in Baja California?
Yes, _____.
Are you going to go to the observatory?
No, _____.
Does Karina work at the observatory?
Yes, _____.

4. occasion occasion

Is this a good occasion to call her?
Yes, _____.
Are you ready for the great occasion?
No, _____.
Do you want to have dinner on another occasion?
Yes, _____.

5. ocean océano

Is this the wonderful Pacific Ocean?
Yes, _____.
Are you going to a beach in the Atlantic Ocean?
No, _____.
Do you like living by the ocean?
Yes, _____.

6. October octubre

Is your birthday in October?
Yes, _____.
Are they going to buy a house in October?

No, _____.
Do you usually go to Cancun in October?
Yes, _____.

7. office oficina

Is this your new office?
Yes, _____.
Are you going to go to the doctor's office?
No, _____.
Do you have an office downtown?
Yes, _____.

8. operation operación

Is this a secret dangerous military operation?
Yes, _____.
Are you going to have an operation?
No, _____.
Do you work on the Desert Operation?
Yes, _____.

9. ordinary ordinario

Is this an ordinary day of your life?
Yes, _____.
Are they having the ordinary problems to
start a business?
No, _____.
Do you like working with ordinary people?
Yes, _____.

P

1. palace palacio

Is that the great Buckingham Palace?
Yes, _____.
Are you working at the king's palace?
No, _____.
Does she play tennis at Royal Palace Hotel?
Yes, _____.

2. panic pánico

Is he feeling panic for the test?
Yes, _____.
Are they feeling panic?
No, _____.
Do you feel panic when you see a rat?

Yes, _____.

3. paper papel

Is this good paper to write?
Yes, _____.
Are you working with white paper?
No, _____.
Do you think this toilet paper is cheap?
Yes, _____.

4. park parque

Is she running at the park?
Yes, _____.
Are you exercising at the park in the
morning?
No, _____.
Does she go jogging at the park at night?
Yes, _____.

5. part parte

Is that part complementary of the red one?
Yes, _____.
Are those the two parts we need to work?
No, _____.
Do you have the parts you are going to work
with?
Yes, _____.

6. patience paciencia

Is he having patience?
Yes, _____.
Are you having the necessary patience for
the class?
No, _____.
Do you think the teacher is having patience
with you?
Yes, _____.

7. penguin pingüino

Is that a penguin emperor?
Yes, _____.
Are those penguins beautiful?
No, _____.
Do you like penguins?
Yes, _____.

8. perfect perfecto (a)

Is this the perfect woman for you?
Yes, _____.
Are you working in perfect synchronization
with her?
Yes, _____.
Do think that's the perfect place for the new
business?
Yes, _____.

9. perfume perfume

Is he wearing that perfume you gave him?
Yes, _____.
Are you going to buy a perfume for your
wife?
No, _____.
Can you smell the perfume that girl is
wearing?
Yes, _____.

10. permanent permanente

Is he making a permanent home in this
country?
Yes, _____.
Are you having a permanent relationship?
No, _____.
Do you work in a permanent shift?
Yes, _____.

11. photo foto

Is this an old photo of you?
Yes, _____.
Are you sorting your wedding photos?
No, _____.
Do have a photo of your girlfriend?
Yes, _____.

1. photographer fotógrafo(a)

Is she a very good photographer?
Yes, _____.
Are they photographers from Brazil?
No, _____.
Do you need a photographer for your prom?
Yes, _____.

2. piano piano

Is he playing the piano very well?

Yes, _____.
Are those the pianos you are going to sell?
No, _____.
Does Roberta play the piano?
Yes, _____.

3. pioneer pionero

Is he a pioneer in that kind of music?
Yes, _____.
Are they pioneers in that area?
No, _____.
Did you speak with the pioneers of the
magazine?
Yes, _____.

4. pirate pirata

Is Captain Hook the pirate in Peter Pan?
Yes, _____.
Is Captain Jack Sparrow a pirate?
No, _____.
Do you like to fight pirates?
Yes, _____.

5. planet planeta

Is the earth a beautiful blue planet?
Yes, _____.
Are Jupiter and Saturn the biggest planets in
the Solar System?
No, _____.
Can you see planet Venus at night?
Yes, _____.

6. planetarium planetario

Is the planetarium a good place to flirt?
No, _____.
Are they visiting the planetarium tomorrow?
No, _____.
Do you like going to the planetarium?
Yes, _____.

7. plans planes

Is this a good plan for the weekend?
Yes, _____.
Are you ready to plan your vacation?
No, _____.
Do you have any plans for tomorrow?
Yes, _____.

91

8. plants plantas

Is this a beautiful plant?
Yes, _____.
Does she have a lot of plants in her house?
No, _____.
Do you like to have plants in the yard?
Yes, _____.

9. plates platos

Is this plate yours?
Yes, _____.
Are those plates over there the ones you need for the reception?
Yes, _____.
Do you have enough plates in the cabinets?
Yes, _____.

10. police policía

Is the police department near your house?
Yes, _____.
Are they good police officers?
No, _____.
Do you think this city has a good police now?
Yes, _____.

11. practice práctica, practicar

Is it important to practice what you learn?
Yes, _____.
Are you practicing your English with American people?
No, _____.
Do you practice any sports?
Yes, _____.

12. prepare (to) preparar

Is he preparing sandwiches for everybody at the seminar?
Yes, _____.
Are you prepared for the test?
No, _____.
Do you prepare your clothes the night before?
Yes, _____.

13. present (to) presentar

Is it important to present a good job?
Yes, _____.
Are you ready to present your school assignment?
No, _____.
Can you present the report on Monday morning?
Yes, _____.

14. presentation presentación

Is this the way you are going to show your presentation?
Yes, _____.
Are they ready for the car presentation?
No, _____.
Do you have a presentation on Wednesday?
Yes, _____.

15. problem problema

Is that a very difficult problem?
Yes, _____.
Are you aware of all the problems that are coming?
No, _____.
Do you solve problems very quickly?
Yes, _____.

16. professional professional

Is he really a professional carpenter?
Yes, _____.
Are your friends professional on their field?
No, _____.
Do you think you are a professional worker?
Yes, _____.

R

1. radio radio

Is he listening to the new radio station?
Yes, _____.
Are they having a presentation on the radio?
No, _____.
Do you have a radio in your bedroom?
Yes, _____.

2. ranch rancho

Is Michael's ranch very big?
Yes, _____.
Are they going to Anita's ranch tomorrow?
No, _____.
Are you planning to buy a ranch?
Yes, _____.

3. really realmente

Is he really Michael Jordan?
Yes, _____.
Are those sandwiches really good?
No, _____.
Do you really want to become a very well prepared bilingual person?
Yes, _____.

4. report reporte

Is this the report you are going to give my boss?
Yes, _____.
Are the reports going to be ready at noon?
No, _____.
Do you fill out reports every week?
Yes, _____.

5. respect respeto

Is respect important among spouses?
Yes, _____.
Are brothers and sisters having respect among themselves?
No, _____.
Do you respect your parents?
Yes, _____.

6. restaurant restaurant

Is Giuseppis a good restaurant?
Yes, _____.
Are they going to meet Ricky Martin at the restaurant in Plaza Rio?
No, _____.
Do you eat in a restaurant every day?
Yes, _____.

7. retire (to) retirar

Is he going to retire after 30 years of working?

Yes, _____.
Are you retiring from the competition?
No, _____.
Do you have plans for retiring?
Yes, _____.

8. reunion reunion

Is this a family reunion/a family gathering?
Yes, _____.
Are these reunions every year?
No, _____.
Does he dream with a reunion with his son?
Yes, _____.

9. rich rico(a)

Is Bill Gates a rich man?
Yes, _____.
Are you a rich person?
No, _____.
Do you want to be a rich entrepreneur?
Yes, _____.

10. rock roca

Is that rock very heavy?
Yes, _____.
Are you taking those rocks to build your foundations?
No, _____.
Do you believe Jesus Christ is the rock of the church?
Yes, _____.

11. route ruta

Is this the main route to the north?
Yes, _____.
Are they taking a different route to the camping?
No, _____.
Do you take the same route to work every day?
Yes, _____.

S

1. second segundo

Is this the second job you have?
Yes, _____.
Are there sixty seconds in one minute?
Yes, _____.
Do you want a second chance for studying a professional career?
Yes, _____.

2. secret secreto

Is she working on a top secret mission?
Yes, _____.
Are there any secrets to be shared about her beauty?
No, _____.
Do you promise not to tell anyone the secret I'm telling you?
Yes, _____.

3. September septiembre

Is it true you went to Cancun in September?
Yes, _____.
Are you going to work in September?
No, _____.
Do have a lot of celebrations in September?
Yes, _____.

4. series serie

Is that the investigation about a series of murders?
Yes, _____.
Are you watching that TV series every night?
No, _____.
Do you have the series numbers of all the computers?
Yes, _____.

5.situation situación

Is this a perfect situation for proposing her?
Yes, _____.
Are you in a very difficult situation?
No, _____.
Do you think being in prison is a bad situation?
Yes, _____.

5. sofa sofá

Is this your favorite sofa?

Yes, _____.
Why are you sleeping on the sofa?
Because_____.
Do you eat in the leaving room on the sofa?
Yes, _____.

6. special especial

Is having dinner with your wife a special moment for you?
Yes, _____.
Are they working on that special project?
No, _____.
Do you think having a child is a special moment in your life?
Yes, _____.

7. statistics estadística

Is this a good statistic for you?
Yes, _____.
Are you working on the productivity statistics?
No, _____.
Do you have the employees' statistics?
Yes, _____.

8. stomach estómago

Is he having an upset stomach?
Yes, _____.
Are you having stomach problems?
No, _____.
Do you have a stomachache?
Yes, _____.

9. study (to) estudiar

Is she studying for her test?
Yes, _____.
Are you studying for the driver's license test?
No, _____.
Do you study every day at night?
Yes, _____.

11.surprise sorpresa

Is he having a surprise birthday party?
Yes, _____.
Are you happy for your surprise promotion?

No, _____.
Do you like giving surprise presents to your children?
Yes, _____.

T

1. telephone teléfono

Is this your telephone number?
Yes, _____.
Are you typing all your friends' telephone numbers?
No, _____.
Do you know who invented the telephone?
Yes, _____.

2. telescope telescopio

Is it true that you have a telescope?
Yes, _____.
Are you looking at the stars with your telescope?
No, _____.
Do you let you children use your telescope?
Yes, _____.

3. television televisión

Is your son watching television (TV) now?
Yes, _____.
Are you going to buy a TV (television) on Sunday?
No, _____.
Do you have a TV in your bedroom?
Yes, _____.

4. terrible terrible

Is a dragon a terrible animal?
Yes, _____.
Are you working on that terrible project?
No, _____.
Did you see the "Terrible" Morales boxing match?
Yes, _____.

5. tomato tomate

Does the spaghetti have tomato sauce?
Yes, _____.
Are you cooking chicken with tomato?

No, _____.
Do you like tomatoes and eggs?
Yes, _____.

6. totally totalmente

Are you totally convinced of working there?
Yes, _____.
Are you totally convinced that your boyfriend is good?
No, _____.
Are you studying medicine totally convinced that you like it?
Yes, _____.

7. tourist turista

Is he a tourist here in Tijuana?
Yes, _____.
Are you going to be a tourist in Mexico City or do you know it very well?
I _____.
Do you work as a tourist guide?
Yes, _____.

8. traffic tráfico

Is traffic terrible in Mexico City?
Yes, _____.
Are there traffic jams in Tijuana?
No, _____.
Do you like the traffic at the border line?
Yes, _____.

9. trap (to) atrapar

Is it difficult to trap a running cat?
Yes, _____.
Are you determined to trap that mouse?
No, _____.
Can you trap flies with two chopsticks?
Yes, _____.

10. triple triple

Is it true that you're getting a triple bonus?
Yes, _____.
Are they going to pay you the triple of your salary from this moment on?
No, _____.
Do give triple tip to waiters who serve you excellently?
Yes, _____.

11. trumpet trompeta

Is that your son's trumpet?
Yes, _____.
Are you learning how to play a trumpet?
No, _____.
Can Tanya play the trumpet very well?
Yes, _____.

12. tube tubo

Is this a dental paste tube?
Yes, _____.
Are you going to buy a tube of candies?
No, _____.
Do you have a tube of aspirin?
Yes, _____.

U

1. uniform uniforme

Is that the uniform you're going to wear at work?
Yes, _____.
Are you going to buy a uniform for your son?
No, _____.
Does she wear a uniform at work?
Yes, _____.

2. union unión

Is the work union located on Palm Ave?
Yes, _____.
Are you going to complain at the labor union?
No, _____.
Do you think *"unity makes strength"*?
Yes, _____.

3. unique único

Is that true your son has a unique talent?
Yes, _____.
Are they having a unique gathering a year?
No, _____.
I think you have a unique talent for music.
Well, thank_____.

V

1. vegetables vegetales

Are vegetables good for you?
Yes, _____.
Are vegetables important for your health?
No, _____.
Do you eat enough vegetables every day?
Yes, _____.

2. version versión

Is that a good version of the Titanic movie?
Yes, _____.
Are you going to watch another version of Frankenstein?
No, _____.
Do you have another version of the facts?
Yes, _____.

3. visit (to) visitor

Is he going to visit his grandmother?
Yes, _____.
Are Michael and Anthony going to visit their mother?
No, _____.
Do you visit your in-laws every week?
Yes, _____.

4. volleyball voleibol

Is volleyball a difficult sport?
No, _____.
Are volleyball players very athletic?
No, _____.
Do you like playing volleyball?
Yes, _____.

5. vote (to) votar

Is it important to vote for president elections?
Yes, _____.
Are you going to vote for him?
No, _____.
Do you vote every three years?
No, _____.

W

1. waterpolo waterpolo

Is water polo your favorite sport?
No, _____.
Are you playing water polo on Saturday?
No, _____.
Do you play water polo when you go on vacation?
Yes, _____.

2. wine vino

Is wine good for your heart if you drink one glass a day?
Yes, _____.
Are you drinking wine with your dinner?
No, _____.
Do you drink wine in parties?
Yes, _____.

X

1. xenophobia xenofobia

Is xenophobia a terrible problem around the world?
Yes, _____.
Are you participating in xenophobic marches?
No, _____.
Do you think xenophobia is good?
No,_____.

2. x-ray rayos x

Is an x-ray examination required for your surgery?
Yes, _____.
Are they going to take you an x-ray photo of your chest?
No, _____.
Do you think x-ray helps to cure illnesses?
Yes, _____.

Y

1. yoga yoga

Is it good to practice yoga?
Yes, _____.
Are you sure you want to do yoga?
No, _____.

Do you like doing yoga?
Yes, _____.

2. yogurt yogurt

Is your yogurt natural or strawberry?
It _____.
Are you going to have yogurt tonight?
No, _____.
Do you like fruit with yogurt and granola?
Yes, _____.

3. yo-yo yoyo

Is this the yo-yo you were looking for?
Yes, _____.
Are those yo-yos over there yours?
No, _____.
Do you like playing the yo-yo?
Yes, _____.

Z

1. zebra zebra

Is a zebra a beautiful animal?
Yes, _____.
How many zebras are there in the zoo?
There are_____.
Do you think zebras are dangerous?
Yes, _____.

2. zero cero

Is it true number zero was invented by Mayas?
Yes, _____.
Is it correct, two minus two equals zero?
Yes, _____.
Do you like temperatures below zero?
Yes, _____.

3. zipper zipper

Can you help me with my zipper, please?
Yes, _____.
Are those zippers made of plastic or metal?
No, _____.
Is the suitcase zipper stuck?
Yes, _____.

4. zone zona

Is this the most exclusive zone in the city?
Yes, _____.
Are you from the nicest zone of Tijuana?
No, _____.
Do rich people live in that zone?
Yes, _____.

5. zoo zoológico

Is San Diego's zoo far from here?
Yes, _____.
Are you going to visit Morelos Park Zoo?

No, _____.
Do you really like going to the zoo?
Yes, _____.

6. zoology zoología

Is zoology part of Biology?
Yes, _____.
Are Karen and Erika going to study zoology?
No, _____.
Do you really think zoology is interesting?
Yes,

IDIOMS

99

TITLES

_____

TITLES

TITLES

TITLES

TITLES

LISTA DE VERBOS (Español)

SIGNIFICADO	PRESENTE	PASADO	P. PARTICIPIO
alimentar	to feed	fed	fed
apostar	to bet	bet	bet
aprender	to learn	learnt / learned	learnt / learned
arrodillarse	to kneel	knelt / kneeled	knelt / kneeled
atrapar	to catch	caught	caught
barrer	to sweep	swept	swept
beber, tomar	to drink	drank	drunk
brillar, dar brillo	to shine	shone	shone
caer	to fall	fell	fallen
cantar	to sing	sang	sung
cavar	to dig	dug	dug
cerrar	to shut	shut	shut
colgar	to hang	hung	hung
columpiar	to swing	swung	swung
comer	to eat	ate	eaten
comprar	to buy	bought	bought
congelar	to freeze	froze	frozen
conocer, encontrarse con	to meet	met	met
conservar, guardar	to keep	kept	kept
convertirse, llegar a ser	to become	became	become
correr	to run	ran	run
cortar	to cut	cut	cut
costar	to cost	cost	cost
crecer	to grow	grew	grown

LISTA DE VERBOS (Español)

SIGNIFICADO	PRESENTE	PASADO	P. PARTICIPIO
criar, reproducirse	to breed	bred	bred
dar	to give	gave	given
dar cuerda	to wind	wound	wound
decir	to tell	told	told
dejar (abandonar)	to leave	left	left
dejar (permitir)	to let	let	let
deletrear	to spell	spelt / spelled	spelt / spelled
desgarrar, derramar lágrimas	to tear	tore	torn
deshacer	to undo	undid	undone
despertar	to wake	woke	woken
dibujar	to draw	drew	drawn
dirigir, liderar	to lead	led	led
disparar	to shoot	shot	shot
dormir	to sleep	slept	slept
empezar	to begin	began	begun
encender	to light	lit	lit
encontrar	to find	found	found
encontrarse	meet	met	met
enseñar	to teach	taught	taught
entender, comprender	to understand	understood	understood
escoger	to choose	chose	chosen
esconder	to hide	hid	hidden
escribir	to write	wrote	written
estar de pié	to stand	stood	stood

LISTA DE VERBOS (Español)

SIGNIFICADO	PRESENTE	PASADO	P. PARTICIPIO
estrujar, retorcer	to wring	wrung	wrung
ganar	to win	won	won
gastar	to spend	spent	spent
golpear, batir	to beat	beat	beaten
hablar	to speak	spoke	spoken
hacer	to do	did	done
hacer	to make	made	made
herir	to hurt	hurt	hurt
Ir	to go	went	gone
jurar	to swear	swore	sworn
lanzar, echar	to throw	threw	thrown
leer	to read	read	read
llevar	to take	took	taken
levantarse, ascender	to rise	rose	risen
mandar, enviar	to send	sent	sent
manejar	to drive	drove	driven
montar	to ride	rode	ridden
morder	to bite	bit	bitten
mostrar, enseñar	to show	showed	shown
nadar	to swim	swam	swum
obtener	to get	got	gotten
oìr	to hear	heard	heard
oler, olfatear	to smell	smelt / smelled	smelt / smelled
olvidar	to forget	forgot	forgotten

LISTA DE VERBOS (Español)

SIGNIFICADO	PRESENTE	PASADO	P. PARTICIPIO
pagar	to pay	paid	paid
pegar	to stick	stuck	stuck
pegar, golpear	to hit	hit	hit
pelear, luchar	to fight	fought	fought
pensar	to think	thought	thought
perder	to lose	lost	lost
perdonar	to forgive	forgave	forgiven
permitir, dejar	to let	let	let
poner	to put	put	put
poner, colocar	to lay	laid	laid
prohibir	to forbid	forbade	forbidden
quemar	to burn	burnt / burned	burn / burned
reventar, explotar	to burst	burst	burst
robar	to steal	stole	stolen
romper	to break	broke	broken
saber	to know	knew	known
sacudir, temblar	to shake	shook	shaken
salir, dejar	to leave	left	left
sangrar, desangrarse	to bleed	bled	bled
sembrar, plantar	to sow	sowed	sown
sentarse	to sit	sat	sat
sentir	to feel	felt	felt
ser, estar	to be (is, are, am)	was, were	been
significar	to mean	meant	meant

LISTA DE VERBOS (Español)

SIGNIFICADO	PRESENTE	PASADO	P. PARTICIPIO
sonar	to ring	rang	rung
soñar	to dream	dreamt	dreamt
soplar	to blow	blew	blown
sostener, agarrar	to hold	held	held
suplicar, abogar	to plead	pled / pleaded	pled / pleaded
tener, haber	to have	had	had
tirar, aventar	to throw	threw	thrown
tomar, agarrar	to hold	held	held
traer	to bring	brought	brought
tumbarse, acostarse	to lie	lay	lain
usar, llevar puesto, calzar	to wear	wore	worn
vender	to sell	sold	sold
venir	to come	came	come
ver	to see	saw	seen
volar	to fly	flew	flown

VERBS LIST (English)

PRESENT	PAST	PAST PARTICIPLE	MEANING
to be	was / were	have/has + been	ser, estar
to beat	beat	beaten	golpear, batir
to become	became	become	convertirse, llegar a ser
to begin	began	begun	empezar
to bet	bet	Bet	apostar
to bite	bit	bitten	morder
to bleed	bled	bled	sangrar, desangrarse
to blow	blew	blown	soplar
to break	broke	broken	romper
to breed	bred	bred	criar, reproducirse
to bring	brought	brought	traer
to burn	burnt / burned	burn / burned	quemar
to burst	burst	burst	reventar, explotar
to buy	bought	bought	comprar
to catch	caught	caught	coger
to choose	chose	chosen	elegir
to come	came	come	venir
to cost	cost	cost	costar
to cut	cut	cut	cortar
to dig	dug	dug	cavar
to do	did	done	hacer
to draw	drew	drawn	dibujar
to dream	dreamt	dreamt	soñar
to drink	drank	drunk	beber

VERBS LIST (English)

PRESENT	PAST	PAST PARTICIPLE	MEANING
to drive	drove	Driven	conducir
to eat	ate	Eaten	comer
to fall	fell	Fallen	caer
to feed	fed	Fed	alimentar
to feel	felt	Felt	sentir
to fight	fought	Fought	luchar
to find	found	Found	encontrar
to fly	flew	Flown	volar
to forbid	forbade	Forbidden	prohibir
to forget	forgot	Forgotten	olvidar
to forgive	forgave	Forgiven	perdonar
to freeze	froze	Frozen	congelar
to get	got	Gotten	obtener
to give	gave	Given	dar
to go	went	Gone	ir
to grow	grew	Grown	crecer
to hang	hung	Hung	colgar
to have	had	Had	tener, haber
to hear	heard	Heard	oir
to hide	hid	Hidden	esconder
to hit	hit	Hit	pegar, golpear
to hold	held	Held	sujetar, mantener
to hurt	hurt	Hurt	herir
to keep	kept	Kept	conservar, guardar
to kneel	knelt / kneeled	knelt / kneeled	arrodillarse
to know	knew	Known	saber
to lay	laid	Laid	poner, colocar

111

VERBS LIST (English)

PRESENT	PAST	PAST PARTICIPLE	MEANING
to lead	led	led	dirigir, liderar
to learn	learnt / learned	learnt / learned	aprender
to leave	left	left	salir, dejar
to let	let	let	dejar
to lie	lay	lain	tumbarse, yacer
to light	lit	lit	encender
to lose	lost	lost	perder
to make	made	made	hacer
to mean	meant	meant	significar
to meet	met	met	encontrarse
to pay	paid	paid	pagar
to plead	pled / pleaded	pled / pleaded	suplicar, abogar
to put	put	put	poner
to read	read	read	leer
to ride	rode	ridden	montar
to ring	rang	rung	sonar
to rise	rose	risen	levantarse, ascender
to run	ran	run	correr
to say	said	said	decir
to see	saw	seen	ver
to sell	sold	sold	vender
to send	sent	sent	enviar
to set	set	set	establecer, poner
to shake	shook	shaken	temblar, sacudir
to shine	shone	shone	brillar, dar brillo
to shoot	shot	shot	disparar, tirar
to show	showed	shown	enseñar

VERBS LIST (English)

PRESENT	PAST	PAST PARTICIPLE	MEANING
to shut	shut	shut	cerrar
to sing	sang	sung	cantar
to sit	sat	sat	sentarse
to sleep	slept	slept	dormir
to smell	smelt / smelled	smelt / smelled	oler, olfatear
to sow	sowed	sown	sembrar, plantar
to speak	spoke	spoken	hablar
to spell	spelt / spelled	spelt / spelled	deletrear
to spend	spent	spent	gastar
to stand	stood	stood	estar de pié
to steal	stole	stolen	robar
to stick	stuck	stuck	pegar (goma)
to swear	swore	sworn	jurar
to sweep	swept	swept	barrer
to swim	swam	swum	nadar
to swing	swung	swung	columpiar
to take	took	taken	tomar, agarrar
to teach	taught	taught	enseñar
to tear	tore	torn	desgarrar, (e) derramar lágrimas (i)
to tell	told	told	decir
to think	thought	thought	pensar
to throw	threw	thrown	lanzar, echar
to understand	understood	understood	entender, comprender

VERBS LIST (English)			
PRESENT	PAST	PAST PARTICIPLE	MEANING
to undo	undid	undone	deshacer
to wake	woke	woken	despertar
to wear	wore	worn	llevar puesto, calzar
to win	won	won	ganar
to wind	wound	wound	bobinar, airear, ventilar
to wring	wrung	wrung	estrujar, retorcer
to write	wrote	written	escribir

At speed™ we believe that by speaking masterfully, you can take your future to a whole new level.

Made in the USA
Middletown, DE
25 June 2021